BLUESOLOGY & BOFELOSOPHY

Poetry & Essays

Mphutlane wa Bofelo

Published by Botsotso Publishing 2008

Box 30952 Braamfontein
2017 South Africa
email: botsotso@artslink.co.za
website: www. botsotso.org.za

ISBN: 978-0-9814068-8-6

We thank the following funders for their support

Cover Design and Layout
Vivienne Preston

Acknowledgement

Dedicated to Dr Phillip Tabane for inspirational, life-giving, soulful and healing music, and to comrade Asha Moodley for her humility, simplicity, selflessness, undying love for people and unflinching passion for life and The Struggle"

CONTENTS

BOOK 1
BLUESOLOGY
POETRY & PROSE

CONTENTS

⭐

BOOK 2
BOFELOSOPHY
ESSAYS & REVIEWS

Book 1

BLUESOLOGY

Poetry and Prose

the blues in her

she writes her anxiety
with needle on wool
lets embroidery sing
blues no composer
can give lyrical tapestry to

if one could live wishes
the story would exit her heart
to live forever on pieces of cloth
decors eternally hanging on boardrooms
dining lounges & bedroom suites
no longer her poor belonging
but stately property of proud collectors
yet the children in the streets
tell her son stories whispered
in households on evening tables
they say grandpa is also daddy
& grandma chose marital bliss
above the health of
her daughter's mind
& the wellbeing of her soul
the verdict is her(e)
knitting is a neurotic
compulsive dealing with repressed
memories of daddy coming from behind

"mama, is it true grandpa was a monster?
the things he did to you, ma
is he in hell, ma?
and grandma,
was she chased from heaven, ma?"

Bluesology

he whistles & hums his burdens
into haunting tunes
surrenders his heart to all ears
his grief sinks in people's minds
a tapestry of the blues buried
within everybody' chests

scribes roll reams of paper
PhD dissertations
on the psycho-metaphysical
dimensions and philosophical
underpinnings of his tunes
the anthropologist graduates cum laude
as an expert in the phonetics and intricacies
of the music of African language
 & a doctor in what-what
on the meaning and origins
                        of Blues
the psychiatry of the Spirituals
the borderline between Jazz & Soul
&   the whys and whatevers of Rhythm and Poetry

his palms caressing
an empty paraffin vessel
he breathes his spirit
in a forsaken hosepipe
empties his lungs
in a lonely bamboo cane
feeds a deserted beer-bottle
with his soul & passersby
with his song-tales-their stories
the musicologist drowns himself
in the acoustics and poetics
of his own voice & swims in sophistic (sem)antics
in an effort to put a tag
on the rhythms and blues
in the jazzy dance of soulful
lips wailing the pounding rap
of rain drops on rooftops of mud-huts

he welcomes the anguish
of the people into his heart
weaves their murmurs and groans
into exhilarating sounds

3.

Dance is...

when the glow of the face illustrates the soul of the mover
when motion is in tune with emotions & the body and the face speak in one voice
when the face talks the speech of the body & the body expresses the talk of the heart
when the face sings the song of bodymotion & bodymovement
expresses the soul behind the face

Me, Barry White? In your dreams

You can move on my dear
No need to look behind
All you will see is your shadow
Do not stress your ears sweetheart
The quietness you hear is for real
Do not listen to your whims darling
There is no whistle calling you back
There are no footsteps behind you
The voice in your ears is not mine
That melody you hear is the hiss of the grass
Maybe it is echoes of the rhymes
I once weaved especially for your ears
You can dance to their beat if you want
A smooth groove and a rhythmic shuffle is no harm
As long as you know these are songs from the past
I am sure you wish I had a mellow baritone
To serenade you all night long
With a sonorous melody
Saying if you can not lie on me
To lie to me will suffice
But no matter how watery
Or lemon-dry they might be

I find nothing seductive
In lips too loose that they utter love for just
Unlike Brook Benton I believe
You can only tell a lie if you live a lie
& most certainly I profess
Only no love in the self and belief in nothing

Nurtures the life of lying
I am sure you still cannot believe
I was able to see your heart was inside his bosom
While your hands toyed with my prick
You may want to know
How my ears could discern
Your cry for him to come inside you
Behind that serenading hum
Urging me to come like thunder
It was that sweeter than always
Melody of your tone
Your voice like the bard's
Talking to a person's heart
Actually speaking the song
Of every lover to any beloved
I will tell you how I came to know
Your mind caressed someone else
Whenever your fingers
Played piano on my body
You were given away
By that gaze as deceptively seductive
As the moon looking like
It is smiling with its looker
While in reality it is
Glowing for everybody

Sleeping beauty

as the invincible tranquility
of the ocean prevails
over the rage of storms
your beauty remains awake
in the deepest of sleep
your awakened face releases
onto the world a smile
that speaks of hopeful
dreams triumphant
above haunting nightmares
every morning I find
you more accomplished
than the day before
every night by your presence
is a blissful experience
in my world there are
no worries over load-shedding
I just cannot afford to wake up
from the clutch of your thighs
into the world of failed power
& limping reality

I feel you

you need not explain your silence
my ears discern the music
of your quietness as good
as your looks caress
me beyond delight
I hear a love declaration
behind your heaving breathing
& quivering mumbling
the same way you were
able to read my lips
as a tongue-tied me
fumbled and wrestled with language
in a fervent plea
for the tongue to transport
deep into your bosom
a telegraph from my heart
how could I not feel
the welcome of your hands
the embrace of your compassion
& now your quiet
loudly beautiful face

Response to a dying lover

you dying when
I am not there
explains your life
when we are together
and how I die without you

this love would not be
if you were to live
in my absence
for you would die in my presence

as for me my love
I have learnt in a special way
it is in dying in your absence
that your omnipresence
in my life manifests itself copiously

this I now know for true
to live life to the full
I have to empty
my heart of too much
of me and refill it
with your everlasting presence

without a blink I declare
the love(r) in me
comes full circle
when I leave
myself behind
& enter you
as nothing but a part
returning to the whole

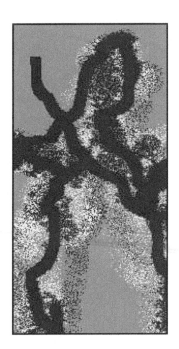

The dance floor is sacred ground, and who am I to tell you this?

(To Molefi "Bobo" Bofelo)

I was going to go
on a long-winded lecture
on the historicity & cultural specificity
of dance as a languageform
involved with the organization
of rhythm and aesthetics…
I was going to go
all pedantic and scholastic
mention a Jay Pather here
quote a Ivaldo Bertazza there
and now and again
without acknowledgement
paraphrase a Danilo Santos de Miranda
& go to town on utilizing
biochemics and the knowledge
of locomotion systems and physiotherapy
to gain a comprehensive grasp of anatomy….
I was going to go all-bookish
and wax philosophical
not necessarily original
on bodylanguage as
a social & cultural construct…
I was going to pretend
I am a choreographer amongst all
& tell you how the physical dimension
heightens a peoples ability

to relate to the worlds…
but how could I sermonize to you
about the potential of dance
to create a collective harmony
as well as bodily express
the collective voice of a people seeking
for a sense of placc in a given space
when with my ears I heard
the audience release
a volcano of claps
by way of ovation
saying the nation sees
its movement out
of the narrow valley of despair
into the vast oasis of hope
in the crazy motion of your tiny feet
soldiering your burdened body
beyond yesterday's ugly scars
above the fresh wounds
of a hobbling today
into the brave world
of the rolling up of sleeves
muddling in the mud
sticking noses in debris
soiling hands with pieces
of derelict and dumped bricks
to build out of the boldness of dreams
a future pregnant with hopes

Durban doccies

North beach

Blue waters, tender sand & cooling air
Tanning bazaars & beer-holes
Bikinis & short-pants, sarongs & liberated tits
No machine-guns here, please lets swim in peace

La Lucia

Gushing springs
Blue lush gardens
Flowery yards
Fresh air & luminous skies
No littering please
This is the north

South beach

Smokey air and fallen dustbins
Blankets peeping through widows
Cigarettes in babies' mouths
Body fluids on the market
Welcome to the South;
Please oil your machine

Scavenging children
A dustbin full of treasures
A packet of chips & sanitary pads
Mzansi for show, hustle for your life

Gateway

Cousin Jack plays clarinet & djembe
Boereqanga & jazzskanda sounds
Musical cocktail for mass appeal
Busking is better than begging

Berea

A bottle of wine & a joint of marijuana
Three poets and one groupie plus rap-reggae
One bed and no condoms-
A threesome haraik

Point road

Itinerant souls, destitute girls & industrial pimps
Hungry stomachs, roaming pricks & roving cash
Free market meets black market

Stanger Street

Famished pants and ravenous mouths
Inventive capitalists and daring girls
Blockbuster movie, full chicken &
Passion kisses on the house

Albert Park

Street kid in a Mercedes Benz
Wealthy hands caressing stinky thighs
Police vans hooting away at metro-blitz speed

Broad Street

Fiery scream
Naked woman
Cops in salute

Aliwal Street

A drunken vagrant
Fly peeping through zip
Giggling passersby

Half-a loaf of bread
Fungi chips and a sniff of glue
Sweet dreams & forgotten scars

Queen Street

Frozen pavement
Two hobos in a tattered box
Smooch for heater
Plastic for soundproof

Grey Street: outside the mosque

A hungry refugee
Snatches a packet of coke
Cans from a delivery lorry
The locals find an opportunity
For jungle justice

West Street

Jalopies bulldoze their way
Through a traffic-jam
Wheels wrestle tired tar-roads

2010 is the hope of the nation
Metro police clear beaches and parks
Of aliens and vagrants and hobos
Streets of hawkers and illegal traders

Mahlathini: Breamar; Umzinto

Children jump in dongas for Jacuzzis
Salivating lips taste after-rain scent
Suck sugar cane for breakfast
Unlucky bums will feel
The crack of the farmer's whip
Older bastards will go to jail

Inanda

He spends the last cent on a bottle of brandy and a packet of cigarettes
Her salary is spent on food and nappies & stuff for the kids
Small change goes to lottery tickets & dreams for the baby on the way
He comes home to a supper of pap and chicken feet
He throws the plate in her face & beats her to pieces
(for wasting money on bloody lotto & stupid things)

Brian Habana scored and the boys partied

The vleis & pap-eating bokke clobbers
Rice & burger munching British paper-lions
Two Pretoria brothers hit the road with a bottle of brandy
Two CZ75 pistols & a plastic tub pregnant with bullets
To celebrate with the centuries old tradition of (Kaffir) hunting

Two Mpumalanga brothers drive to Gauteng
Three small children and a woman in the backseat
Hearts filled with dreams and hopes of reunion with relatives
But Black is still a hunter's favorite game in 21st century SA

As gunfire rains on a family & bullets cut a boy's throat
White boys make a u-turn to resume the hunting
A father shows his wife photos of their dead child on a cell phone
While the IMF & the World Bank pop sherry & rum
A toast to Africa's greatest democracy

All power to some people

The budget allocated to the arts centre is R2 million
All staff is voluntary, the director is a casual
Community groups and private bodies pay for functions
The big corporates throw their bit
The audit statement is incomplete
The accountant died in the Kenya plane crash
What's certain is that nothing is left for this financial year
The deficit is R 200 000
Sixty thousand was spent on special occasions
Tenders went to the director's spouse
The cousin was a shareholder
The mayor was a silent partner
The girl friend a consultant…
Forget about sexually transmitted diseases
The limelight is on sexually transmitted economic empowerment
Bags falling from owners into skillful hands guarantee no loot
Self-made blindness & bowl-hands attract few coins from good Samaritans
Pick-pocketing & begging is so out of trend *(?)
Creative fundraising is the current
When one cannot afford not to hope that one day
He or she will be at the top & all worries will be gone
There is no moment to care about the missing link in the pyramid scheme
With the nation so in need of heroes
The cheer crowd ready for hire
The media starving for scoops
The possibility of a corruption trial
Presents an opportune moment
To be a star of the moment
Newsmaker of the year
There is no room for losers here
The cost of being a hero is zero
If your trade denies you the chamzer award
You can try your luck in the controversy bid
Anyway better be a mogoe of the decade
Rather than come out of the celebrity race with nothing
You do not need to be grandiloquent
There are many ways to explain your actions
If you are a Kwaito-star turned TV personality-cum UN ambassador
The paparazzi are jealous of you for eclipsing
The limelight from them in their own territory

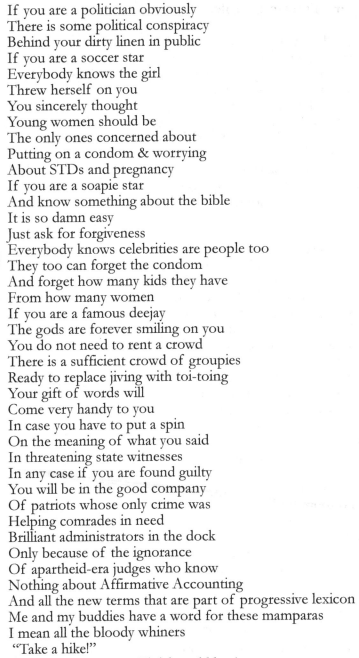

If you are a politician obviously
There is some political conspiracy
Behind your dirty linen in public
If you are a soccer star
Everybody knows the girl
Threw herself on you
You sincerely thought
Young women should be
The only ones concerned about
Putting on a condom & worrying
About STDs and pregnancy
If you are a soapie star
And know something about the bible
It is so damn easy
Just ask for forgiveness
Everybody knows celebrities are people too
They too can forget the condom
And forget how many kids they have
From how many women
If you are a famous deejay
The gods are forever smiling on you
You do not need to rent a crowd
There is a sufficient crowd of groupies
Ready to replace jiving with toi-toing
Your gift of words will
Come very handy to you
In case you have to put a spin
On the meaning of what you said
In threatening state witnesses
In any case if you are found guilty
You will be in the good company
Of patriots whose only crime was
Helping comrades in need
Brilliant administrators in the dock
Only because of the ignorance
Of apartheid-era judges who know
Nothing about Affirmative Accounting
And all the new terms that are part of progressive lexicon
Me and my buddies have a word for these mamparas
I mean all the bloody whiners
 "Take a hike!"
                    Finish and klaar!

Hot Coals

in his dreams he can read lyrics of the wind's song
in his vision he verbalizes the harmony
of the hiss of the grass and the hum of the river
on the palms of leaves he reads the future
in people's faces of he sees their fate
in the rattle of the bones he hears
the voice from beyond
a flurry of images invades his wake
floodgates of emotions pulsate
through every bit of limb and body
a hurricane of thoughts whirls in his brain
a cacophony of sounds frolics in his head
an acoustic of heart-beats bumps and grinds in his chest
a rocking chorus pumps and grooves in his heart
an incessant melody rings in his ears
his is to disown the beat of the drum in his ears
let go of the strum of the guitar in his eardrum
disclaim the tune of his heartbeat
release the song in his heart
give it to the people
let the beat be theirs to claim
the vibe theirs to own

keeping the endurance needed
to answer to this call
to let go of one's voice &
make it the peoples
is like holding hot coals

Cool Types

their blood flows with order
their flow is in sync with the current
their hearts know what's in the mix
their minds never bother about what's out
their speak is never off track
their walk is forever in trend
they know the colors of the season
they command the numbers at every event
they master the calendar of events
their noses discern the flavor of the moment
in their ears pump the sounds of the time
on stage lives the world of their dreams
    oh dear!
how their flow faints when the current ceases to run
how they their currency deflates when the trends are no longer current
how they lose their speech when they don't have a track to follow
how their voices drown when they are not in the mix
how they fumble when they have to flow under no order
how they stumble when they have to walk without the crowd
how they huff and falter when they have to make their own sounds
how their bodies tremble when they have no queue to walk in
how they lose their cool when they have to move without a cue

Caring for Black Labour

To drown all your sorrows and refresh your wretched and wrecked body, forget about **Laugh it Off's** *insinuations that this beer- and the wealth accrued from it- is built on* **black labour** *and that our noble social responsibility programmes are at best the results of* **white guilt** *and at worst a mere public relations exercise…At least we know that after all the hard-work of the day and the physical depravity you suffer in the townships and rural areas, you deserve to find mental solace in a glass of extra-matured, carefully brewed beer for quick and ultra effects*

At the end of the day …   The union and the employers agree
In the interest of economic growth
The workers will be retrenched
And then re-enter the job market
Via sub-construction consortiums
Owned by former shop stewards
Turned avid entrepreneurs

More rewarding.

After a glass & few puffs
The casual worker counts
The few days left before
The 'piece job' is over

Refreshing …….

When the sun goes down
Mqwathi takes a cold shower
Jumps into bed
After shouting instructions
To his wife and kids
To tell the shebeen queen
He is doing overtime

Extra digit

Another opening and a new beginning
A new face and another seeker
Extra digit to multitudes
A crucial reinforcement to the left
A new voice and fresh breath
Fresh legs and inquisitive hands
Searching and questioning eyes
Open mind and discerning ears
Sensitive body and resonant screams
Quick reflexes and unrestrained cries
A vital additional voice for the left

(Dedicated to my son, Goitsemodimo-born with an extra digit on the left hand)

She came and the boy became a man

She came in the morning
Her face wearing the look of anticipation
Icebreaker smile appealing:
"I am knocking at the door of your heart
Look at me with your eyes and you will see
My back is as broad as my smile
My hands speak the tenderness of my heart
Years of experience are written in my moves
My footprints are carved on city pavements
The tunes I hum are on the lips of many babies
Many households sing my songs
Just wait and you will see
The boy will speak the melodies of the birds
And dance the movement of sea waves"
She returned the next day and the day after
Today the baby boy is a grown man
Singing songs of the mountain
Articulating the joys and sorrows of coming of age

Hot Types

Let us not even begin
to define the hot type
suffice to just say
when a coal is Lebo Mathosa hot
iron melts thousands kilos away its reach *(?)
and when a trouser is blazing
with Fela Kuti passion
groupies reach orgasm
before they touch it

If you were to break the legs
of a Brenda Fassie
or clip the wings of a Billie Holiday
she would still find a way
to break a leg and spread her wigs
with her heart on the mic
her soul moving her skirt
her body revealing her spirit
her middle finger
declaring a resonant"F…off!"
to whoever dares to press down
the daredevil spirit
of a being too hot
to be anything except
HOT!

We are talking about the REAL *hot types*
they speak in tune with the play of their bodies
 their egos go with the
      raucous stream of
                        their desires
their feet follow
    the track of their passions
           their spirits flow
                   with the current
 of their feelings

their heads bow
        to the craving of the flesh

  the spontaneous ooze of their carnal blood rains against the censor's razor

when the lights go off they let body current ignite the spark of fire
out of the rule of their dreams they establish a regime of no systems no restraints
off the track they walk on grass to carve new paths
when the chorus dies they find their voice in solo
they discover the centre of tomorrow on the sidelines of society

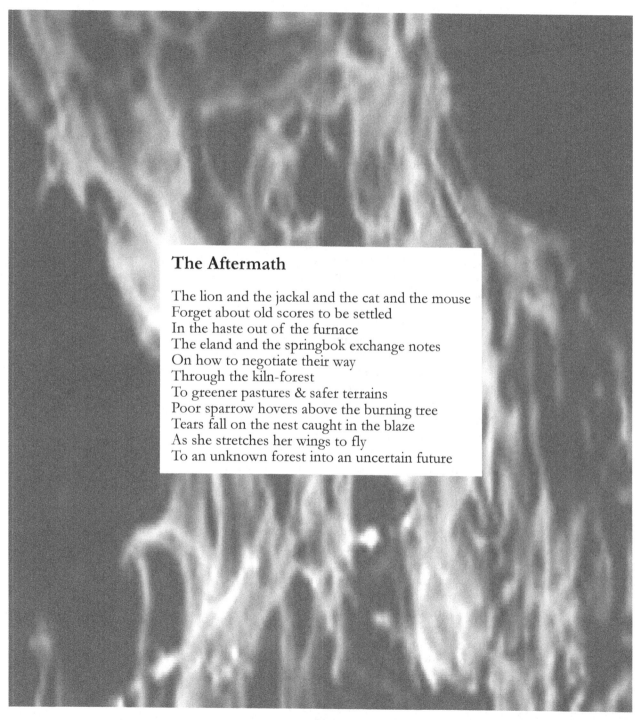

The Aftermath

The lion and the jackal and the cat and the mouse
Forget about old scores to be settled
In the haste out of the furnace
The eland and the springbok exchange notes
On how to negotiate their way
Through the kiln-forest
To greener pastures & safer terrains
Poor sparrow hovers above the burning tree
Tears fall on the nest caught in the blaze
As she stretches her wings to fly
To an unknown forest into an uncertain future

At the Barbershop

"These sounds take me home
I see myself sitting in a chair
Drinking homebrewed & eating homegrown
I mean true fruit & wholesome vegetables"
"Yeah! These tunes take me back in time
When we partied in our own lingo
With unrestrained laughter and chatter
Before the music gave way to the guns' clatter
And merry dances were replaced by the peoples' scatter."
The stereo blasts sounds of Papa Wemba
Kofi Olumide or Kanda Bongo man
This proud Mzansi for sure fellow
Cares not much about the difference
As long as his hair is well done
& his trousers are the proper cut
The musical taste and dreams of
A poor barber and a lousy tailor
& their rattle about the woes
Of war and the worries and bothers of exile
Not his baby to cuddle
He has an important engagement at La Lucia
It is prudent to be punctual
At tender presentation meetings
Needless to talk about
The importance of proper attire
Clothing is after all the face of a person
& making money is truly the mark of a true man

He ogles the barber and the tailor
As they groove to the music of their country
Chanting names of friends and relatives who
Died en route to the land of gold and rand
Their counting of the number
Of acquaintances killed by xenophobes
In the greatest democracy in Africa
Makes him squirm and wriggle
"My change, please! Make it snappy,
I have a business meeting"
He conceals his snarl with a partial-smile
And turns to his countrymen in the queue
Muttering stuff that sparks guttural mirth

Dear parents

For your every touch, push and pull through the up-and down- swings of this life-journey
For the gentle caress and soothing lullaby
For the emphatic listening to my cries
For hearing the call in my screams
For your compassionate response to my calls
For the warm and assuring hugs
For your tender hold that injected impulse in my step out of crawling
For the patience you displayed whenever I missed the steps
For the push and cheer you gave whenever I succumbed to fear and fatigue
For the pull-up and pep-up whenever I seemed to be discouraged by falling
For the direction you offered whenever I veered off the way
For sharing your stories and experiences openly
For making me aware of the wisdom of learning from experience
For showing me how to live by convictions
For teaching me how to teach by actions
For educating me that making choices in life saves one from living by chance
For often returning with mercy whenever I strayed
For showing me the way of the Most Gracious and Most merciful
For all the moments of being
For all memories of belonging
For this time and this moment
For your intimate presence and shouldering support
For being with me this day
For the pleasure of knowing you will be there always
This is just to let you know
I know that I am and will be always your child
For you and for the bright future of your grandchildren and this nation
I will never let the child inside me die
For I know I will only be a better parent
If I remember the child you wanted me to be

The story told

June's baby died because
Infant meat whets the appetite
Of granny the wizard
Its mother is actually not dead
The old witch never touches a broom
But her house and yard are sparkling clean
At the unholy hours of the night
You can hear her furniture dancing
A grass cutter moaning on her lawn
June's husband was failed by his heart
Seeing his wife and child die
At the hands of his own mother
Punctured him to pint-size
As for his diminutive
Former voluminous mistress
She's dying from food poisoning
Everybody knows she started spewing blood
After eating food at June's husband's funeral
Her celebrity husband has lost weight
Due to being overstressed
By too many performances
And the invasion of his life
By the Peeping Toms & prying cameras

Verwoed is Black: Biko is on holiday
(With apologies to Mpho Ramaano)

Alexandra is up in flames
Black flesh is the fuel
Voices celebrating
The cheapness of black life
Belt out not the erstwhile notorious die stem
But the now in/famous mshini wam
Hands baying for Kaffir blood
Raise not the swastika & the fier kleur
But the clenched fist & the rainbow flag
This time the K word is not
An Afrikaans version
Of the Arabic heathen
But our own African
Fervent articulation
Of negrophobia
A raging hatred
Of any reminder
Of how Black our continent is
Not to mention our deliberate choice
To forget to remember
How our ancestors hailed
From the Centre of Africa
And found the First People of Azania
The men among men
Moving rocks to speak the language of art

It was only yesterday
When the whole world
The greens and the reds and the pink
All shades of convictions and ethics
In a literal and symbolic exposition

Of the existence of three worlds in one nation
And the yawning chasm in the quality of life
Of the poor and the rich in this great country
Distinguished for its penchant for mix-masala
Marched to opulent Sandton
Via muddy terraces & falling shacks
Academic lenses, activist eyes
Tourist cameras and researchers' videos
Zooming on Alex children
Licking dry fingers for lollipop
& Jukskei River humming a distressed
Elegy to people who
Fear summer for torrents
Of rain filtering in
Like water through a sieve
And cringe at the approach
Of the winter that adds coldness to the long list
Of the natural and nurtured
Hostilities against the poorest of the poor
But now the poor of Alex
Bay for the blood of the poor of Zimbabwe/ Nigeria/Congo/ Somalia
Little urchins are verbal assassins
The target of their obnoxious vitriol is not the system
As we tremble in worship of the establishment
That forever quarantines us on the periphery
And shudder to confront the demons within us
We scrape our mother's wombs for new soft targets
To turn our rage against our newly found national scapegoat.
......AMAKWEREKWERE

wisdom lost

there is no book
in the whole world
to teach new tricks
to an old dog
but a wise dog knows
when old tricks are done
& when new rules will do

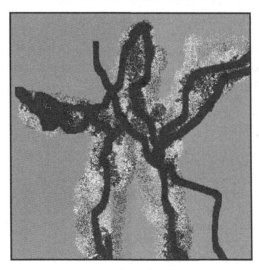

The Shopping mall Revolution: Press clippings

Activists are trapped to old and tired dictums
Jailed in the prison of their rhetoric
They fail to behold the new face of the struggle
And see the strides already made
In the second phase of the revolution:
Black (m)asses doing it in suburban clubs
Che Guevara smiling on youngsters' chests
Baggy pants dancing in corporate boardrooms
Dreadlocks and Afros riding A4's and 4 X 4's
These radicals must admit
This revolution has made milestones:
You can now eat ting and malamogodu in Sandton
Make a date with Gerald Sekoto in Rosebank
Go home with designer under-wears bearing the name Biko
Let's stop whining and ship? **(sip?)** sherry for the new generation
For turning images into rebuilding stones
The vinyl is powered with revolutionary speak
Poetic voices quote bits and pieces from **I write what I like**
Paraphrases are movie titles

This is but the beginning of a great reawakening
Young people search for their identity in cyberspace
Elders log onto the net to look for their family tree
Families surf the web for their totems
Children peruse tabloids for role models
Role models take shopping for therapy
Hospitals dispense panados for every illness
Garlic and beetroot a panacea for all diseases
The president smokes a pipe for relief
Poets find symbolic meaning in the lighting of the pipe (and the ashes of the tobacco)

They say the sleeping giant shall rise from the quagmire
Like a phoenix from the ashes to reclaim
Its rightful place as the pathfinder and explorer of the new

The world is left bedazzled and befogged
As the great son of the soil leads the pioneering process
With the rediscovery of the healing power of water
& the unearthing of the precautionary value of a post-coital shower
Cynics must be freed from the chronic illness of pessimism and admit
This newly born nation has matured:
Young lions have grown into corporate executives
Now weeping for the loss of a business compatriot
The first among the few to actualize
The ideal of a patriotic bourgeoisie
Putting his wallet on his lip in service of Broad Based BEE
The government is also in mourning
In view of the growing Afro-pessimism
The demise of one more Afro-optimist is too painful a loss to bear
Cultural activists painfully ponder about the future
Of the continent's only awards for the visual arts
The skulls in the closet leave tongues dancing
CEO's and ministers are running on endless errands
To cover their heads over the shame and revelation
Their asse(t)s are wrapped in stolen Rands

Freedom day provides an ample opportunity
For escape from the world of everyday experience
Into the world of theatrical celebrations
Pop music and Kwaito beats
Punctuated with political speeches
For the masses to drown their sorrows
In the wine of rhetoric and the opium of freedom songs
As the president mentions in passing
The death of a struggle hero
In the middle of a long winded speech
Promising a season of more promises
Leaving commentators too busy pondering
Their future in government or business

Hurrah to an easy-forgetting nation
Trading memory for amnesia
Choosing selective remembering
Embracing convenient omission
Thriving on a chequered remembrance

Importing gods and heroes
Selling ancestors for pop stars
Endless probabilities of a shopping mall revolution
A shopping-mall-generation opting
For consumption above production
A born-free breed fostered in the intensive care unit
Of the global market village
Nurtured on an African Renaissance
Born and bred in South Africa
Like Nandos burning with ambition
To spread flames across the world
Like SABC exporting to the rest of Africa
An imported adolescent culture
Born in the belly of the beast
Spawning airheads
Full of meat and empty of soul
Slick voices minus wit and humour
Pretty faces hot for television and radio but brainy for none
Namedroppers and stunt-makers
Riding the bandwagon of hedonism
Celebrities in public circulation by virtue
Of topping the list in sexcapades
Public brawls and drug addiction
Staged rehabs and rehearsed relapses....
Scramblers for the throne of pop deity
Divas parading pomp and grandiose
(Lying low on the divinity and humility part of the deal)
Godfathers who are makers of babies and fathers to none...

Commentators with the left hand on the situation &
The right one on bank statements
Scholars with a leg in academia and an eye on government posts
Governors with one eye on administration and another on business
Cut and paste academics regurgitating exhausted dictums
Revolutionaries dancing in a post-struggle orgy
Photo kisses of a dead patriotic bourgeoisie
An economic Empire built on broken-down transactions
The legacy of kleptomania sanctioned by political correctness
Looting decorated with the right political connections
Political careerism and self-enrichment rewarded
By deployment to the corporate sector
Forced resignation complemented by golden handshakes…

Public-bought private jet globetrotting on a shopping spree
Classical music blasting in the air
Delicacies in the sky
Expensive shit over seas
Exotic Arabian nights
Air-conditioned sleep
Eastern delights and designer garbs
Merry-ride on sand dunes
Political arithmetic counting millions as a pittance
Whitewashing, wishy-washy explanations
Blurring the distinction between a holiday trip
& a business assignment

Poetry under spotlight

Writing for live camera-action
Lenses zoomed on the face
Sound-effect on the breath and the silence
Slow-motion hands caressing the goatee
Premeditated pensive poise
Spotlight on every speck of motion
Inquests into the gaze of the eyes
Gropes for cues into the poet's thought
As if a poem is a psychometric window
Into the poet's state of mind
But poetry flows from the heart
And no microscopic measure
Shall dare approximate
The depth and state of the heart

The killer within

1
Like fleas cherish a sluggish
Surreptitious ruin of their habitat
Anger relishes a slothful
Demolition of the heart that harbours it
2
Just as ants wage a silent
War of slow destruction
To trounce colossal mountains
Vengeance leisurely chews
The chest that gives it homes
3
The rapturous whispers of the ego
Delude the flattered self that
The other is the victim
Of vitriolic outburst & retributive violence
Whilst iblis disguised as anger
Joyously throttle the human from within

The prophet's cure for anger

Vacate the terrestrial zone
Move out of yourself
Close your eyes from the flattery of the ego
Recline, loll on the carpet
Let it lull you away from the self
Launch into the outlook of the world
Through the view of the other person
See how ordinary your fears and loves are
And realize how universal your need
For dignity and respect and your want
For love and understanding are

Graffiti at The Bat

You may say it is an illusive
Caressing of bruised ego
The wealthy voice of the indigent
Shouting tongue-in-cheek on the wall:
"Rich people are so poor
The only thing they have is money"
For those who hear with the heart
The gospel on the wall is clear
Poor people are so rich
They can read the poverty in riches

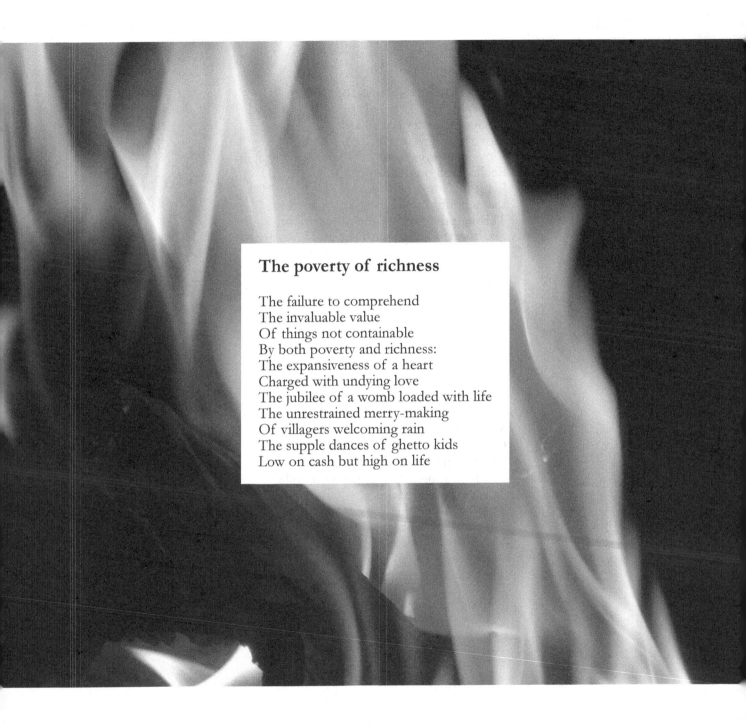

The poverty of richness

The failure to comprehend
The invaluable value
Of things not containable
By both poverty and richness:
The expansiveness of a heart
Charged with undying love
The jubilee of a womb loaded with life
The unrestrained merry-making
Of villagers welcoming rain
The supple dances of ghetto kids
Low on cash but high on life

Man for all seasons

I put a tie on my khaki suit, take off my JR hat, ponder for a little while, put it on again, wear my HIV/AIDS ribbon, loudly singing the English, Isizulu and Sesotho parts of the national anthem, and saying aloud the greetings in these languages to see how far I've gone with working on my accent. For the first time after forty years of its existence, *Orange Vaal Kultuur Fees* will be open to all cultures and races and I am the master of ceremonies (these days it is called program director); mine is a task insurmountable. The folks understand the realities- that it is mission impossible to sell the Orange, that is an all white cultural festival, to the emergent Rainbow Nation that has become a part of the Global Village. They realize that a multiracial festival will be more sellable and that we need a few black faces to be able to court corporate and government funding. Yet I still need to assuage their fears that our culture is about to be thrown in the dumping grounds of history. On the other hand I need to make the whole country believe that ours is not token transformation. My own personal image is at stake here. I have to assure the guys that I'm still worth my salt and at the same time show the government and the international community that the *Orange Vaal Kultuur Gemeenskaap* - the name change debate is still coming - is committed to transformation. I definitely need to master the art of uttering statements with a multiplicity of meanings and saying things that mean different things to different people, depending on where they stand and what blinkers they wear.

I really have to dress up for the occasion and be everything to everybody. Thus far I've been equal to the task. The khaki is for the folk, the hat is for the crown-as you know we are back in the commonwealth and the sun shall never set on the British Empire - the tie is for civility, the ribbon is a political statement, the singing of the official national anthem is as right a thing to do like paying your television license and the multi-lingual greeting is as politically correct as they come.

 I can handle situations like this because I am a practical man for whom convenience is the only dogma and existential conditions the supreme reality in life. For me the world is my place as long as I am able to be the right person at the right moment and assume the correct role at the right place in time. I have seen and done it all and like a cockroach I have survived earthquakes and all sorts of storms. In South West Africa I was Mr. Government, in Angola I was a hired gun, in Mozambique I supplied the guns, at Quito Cunavale I was the fuel, in Kwazulu -Natal I fuelled the fire; in Boipatong I provided the fuel.

Tonight I am the program director. My goal is reconciliation; my message is to forgive and forget the skeletons in the closet, to bury the past and its woes, to celebrate the present and its scandals and to be ready to feed on the carcass tomorrow. For me, the man of all times and citizen of the Global Village, there are no fixed roles and rigid rules but the universal law of convenience and gain, or profit as it is called today. I ask one and only one question: What is in it for me? The choice to be a troublemaker or trouble-shooter depends on my gain/profit/convenience/comfort/security.

I have been a dove in times of peace and a hawk in times of war and I have been a hawk in peace times and a dove in war times. What is convenient and profitable for me at a particular point in time and place informs my decision to choose whether I should make peace or war.

Today I am in my jeans and takkies and clad in one of the dashikis I bought in the DRC the other day. I made sure that I chose the one with the gold and black colors, and fit it with a green polo-neck jersey. My appearance must make a statement, even before I open my loud mouth to make a presentation to the local government on why my Afrique Events Company should be awarded the tender to host the official Ten Years of Democracy celebrations. Everyone knows I am the most appropriate guy for the job. I provide all the freebies at the main rallies and events of every important political party, community organization and professional body known in this province, print free T-shirts for them, and generously contribute to the election drives of all the major political parties -anonymously, of course. I know the rule of this business, my man. Flexibility, versatility, ambiguity and anonymity are the trump cards. Fixed identities and grand master plans do not work here.

I know this game like the palm of my hand because I've been through rainstorms, thunder and-dust-and-bullets storms and all sorts of cataclysmic explosions as I traversed deserts, plains and mountainous areas in the line of duty. In Biafra I was underground, in new York I am undercover, in Zaire I worked with the government, in Congo Brazzaville I was with the rebels, in the Democratic Republic of Congo I was in all sides, in Rwanda I was behind the scenes, in Johannesburg I am a poet, in Paris I am a pimp, in Kabul I am in the oil industry, in Somalia I was a peace-broker, in Baghdad I am a constructor and the future for me is as clear as clouds, in Zimbabwe I was in transit, in Equatorial Guinea I was in mining, and tomorrow I am going to Lebanon in transit to Israel as a Road Map consultant.

Soapie

For our story to continue the character and the author must die because if they live they will spoil everything by dying, thereby causing our story to die. The author is a man and men cannot live forever, the character is a product of a man's mind, observations, fantasies and imagination, and human beings impose mortality, fallibility and all other qualities they possess upon everything they make.

For the sake of the continuity of our story, the author and the protagonist were long dead before the story began, or the story began long before the narrator and the character were certified dead and reborn. For fact not to disguise itself as fiction and fiction not to call herself non-fiction, the narrator and the protagonist, the author and the character is one person, and the former dies for the latter to be born.

Unlike in many stories where the narrator's voice dominates, suffocates and throttles voices of the characters, in our story the narrator kills himself to give life to the character and every time the protagonist dies the author comes to life so that he may die for the protagonist to be born again. Whenever the author lives, the character dies, whenever the narrator dies, the protagonist comes to life and vice versa. From the ashes of the author the protagonist rises to life. From the character's life comes the death of the author, and from the death of the character comes the life of the author.

For the sake of keeping this story alive, there shall be no time limits and spatial configuration. For our story to live forever there shall be no order. There shall be no tolerance for grammatical regulations and all rules and laws under the sun. There shall be no regard for literary conventions and no need for poetic license because nothing shall be disregarded and nothing shall need a license to be said and done.

For our story to be real-life it has to be a chaotic order/ organized chaos. Formlessness and formatlessness shall be the very form and format of our organized disorder- our story cum high-story-cum-his-story-cum-her- story-cum-your-and-my- story stroke me story slash mystery. There shall be no time and space, no sequence, no plot and no border between nothingness and somethingness. Being shall be non-being, life shall be death and vice-versa...

Guluva's story is my story and yours .Our story is every day's story. I am Guluva. I am you because I am because you are. You are Guluva. You are I because I am because you are. Guluva is because we are, therefore we are all Bo-Guluva. Everybody is we because we are because of everybody. I am everyone and our story takes place wherever everybody is. Every one is part of the story, every place is the setting of our story, every time is the period of our story because no matter what / never mind why our story takes place anytime/\ every time anywhere every where, anyhow / every how...

I danced with my shadow last night or last night I walked with my shadow and she taught me there is a dance in each and every ordinary step I take each and every moment of my life. That each and every footstep leaves behind a footprint that is a signature and a mark imprinted on the pages of history. I am gray with envy at my shadow for all the privilege to walk through the slippery, rough, sloppy, mountainous, steep, shallow, narrow, dark, deep terrenes with me without having to endure all the pain and agony that sometimes goes with it. What do you tune man? Who said it is cool to be a shadow of a failure. What do I have to say when I meet other shadows? That I am a shadow to a man afraid to look at his own shadow, lest he see himself in it and confirm the difficult to swallow reality that he is nothing but a simple ordinary part of the ordinary mass that matters only because there is a need to add statistics and figures to the national flag, the anthem and the throne. I am talking non-sense. Which shadow has a good story to tell? I am crying that I am on the road on burning sands in dusty streets on rainy days in cold nights, but that shadow yonder complains about belonging to a fat forever-eating always-farting big-shot who lives for strolling half-naked on the beaches of the world with no need to sleep or dream, but a reason to keep wake all night for the fear of waking up to find the world standing on new foundations with no rich and no poor and no three worlds nor clashing civilizations but one world and one humanity one destiny and one future.

What songs shall we sing at the gathering of the shadows of the world? We are shadows of the peasants laboring for peanuts under the sweltering sun and shadows of the propertied that get ill from idling. We are the shadows of poor who produce without consuming and die from not eating and shadows of the rich who consume without producing and die from overeating. When we ultimately meet to discuss the future without shadowhood or the future of shadows, if shadows really do have a future, what shall be our clarion call, which marching-songs shall propel us forward? Which dictums shall we chant and which slogans shall we shout? "Shadows of the world unite against the shadow of the self; you have nothing but your shadow status to loose and wholeness to gain." In which language shall we sing the song? What shall be our lingua franca when the universal language of struggle has become empty jargon and theatric rhetoric? "Shadows of the world, rise up to find a new language for the world without shadows. You have your self to lose and yourself to regain in a world without shadows."

Last night I visualized Mmanyeo among the audience in the theatre. I saw her radiating face vanquishing artificial light, and her eyes speaking love, peace and tranquility. She listened, laughed and cheered and danced and cried with the people moved by my poetic talk. She stood up with them as they gave me a standing ovation. I liked the way she smiled, standing in the crowd, composed like a poem, not driven crazy by the pride of having the key and lock to the heart of the charmer of the masses- the poet. She did not boastfully parade her connections with the hero of the moment, she patiently waited as admirers saluted, hugged and kissed their griot. She hungrily but patiently waited for her time to give the biggest and warmest of the hugs- the hug only she could give. When the time arrived we escaped the tyranny of society and dwelt in the paradise of love and affection. We blocked our ears and our bodies heard. We closed our eyes and our bodies saw. We shut our mouths and our bodies spoke. We ventured into the unseen, heard the unheard and spoke the unspoken and unspeakable.

Tonight I ascend the stage eaten by the anguish and torment of feeling Mmanyeo's absence in the theater, and bitten by the thought that this could herald the beginning of her eternal absence in my life. Hope is dead, killed by a nightmarish one-night stand. As my time to take the stage arrives, a friend if mine urges me forth: "Speak brother, you are the voice and hope of the nation! Artists burnt the fires of hope at the darkest of hours in the history of humankind. Raise your poetic voice and ignite the fires of hope, brother man" He is not aware that he is speaking to a ghost - a man chewed by the anguish of feeling nothing is left to live for, after being betrayed by a woman that he had come to believe is part of him.

For days I've been fantasizing about the good time I will have with Mmanyeo after my graduation as a community theatre ambassador. We've been spending hours on the phone, singing our undying love for each other and how we will tear each other's clothes off when we meet. Last week I sent her money for transport to come to the graduation, and yesternight she confirmed that at six o'clock she will be in a Welkom-to-Vereeniging Taxi. Suddenly she called me this morning to tell me she cannot come. From her sobbing voice I could detect something is eating her. Finally she managed to break the news. She's carrying another man's child and did not have the courage to tell me all these days that we've been making love to each other over the phone. She met this guy at a friend's party and woke up the following day between his legs. She swore by all the living and dead things that she did not love the man and could not imagine herself getting to love him, let alone marry him.

…
"I rather be dead than live with him
He is not the man in my heart I know the man of my dreams
If this fault means I lose

The man I really love I rather be alone
For the rest of my life
My baby will be my only companion
I shall teach her to hold on to dreams
Be careful of the choices to make
One little act can make
Or unmake one's life"

What is to blame? Is it fate or the distance between us?

I am on the platform. I talk beauty, humanity, love and compassion. My talk moves the people. They are on their feet. "Speak brother man, your voice is our voice, our cry is in your voice." I like and love the beauty in their faces ...the glow of hope. But there is a face, smile and hug I miss. Will I see Mmanyeo's face again? Shall I feel the warmth of her hug again? Shall I still see her beauty when we meet, one of these blessed days?
The cry keeps ringing in my ears:

"Please forgive me
You are the only one I love
You revealed to me
The lover behind a man
Yet I failed you terribly
Give a second time please
I will use every second of it
To restore what we had"

"Good morning sunrise
Today I greet you not with murmurs
Whispered vows over symphony screams
There is no morning bite
To greet your exotic rays of light
Only dark eyes mourning the death
Of the spark that lit the fire
Sad tears at the break
Of vows taken by the break of dawn
Shall I sing a dirge?
For a union that embodied
The beauty of human relationships
But was killed by human folly?
Good morning dawn-break
Remember the action
Motion pictures we imposed on you
Intimate never-ending oaths
We compelled you to be a witness to
They have gone with the night
Snatched by the brutal darkness
That staged a coup over sunrise
To make sunshine my sunset
Good morning harsh reality
Suddenly I wake up
From the slumber land of blind love
Actions last for but a while
Words are said but in a moment
But the consequences of the actions
And the memory of the words
Last beyond today, tomorrow and the day after tomorrow
Good morning beloved day
Tomorrow is yet another day
Its sunrise might be my sunshine
Or perhaps your sunset
Shall be the rising of my star"

How many times was I born, how many times was I dead, how many times was I reborn? How many times was I mourned, how many times did I rise, how many times was I buried, how many moments was I reborn? I long to return to the time and place before I came into the dark about who I am, and where I was before I came to be unsure that who I am is the real me, and began to wonder whether what I am is all I could be.

How come it is such a painful exercise for me to remember the last time I smiled and the place where I had my last cry or, at least, the last time I saw a face smile at me, or heard some voice sing and cry for me? How the hell do I count the times and remember the places when I cannot recall the faces that smiled when I was born and the eyes that released tears when I died?

A space becomes a place because of beings that people it and people become known because they have faces. Faces are faces because they can be seen by the naked eye, and eyes are eyes because they can see. What is a place without a people, what is a is a person without a face, what is face without eyes, and what are eyes without tears of joy and tears of sorrow?

What is a person without a people, what are a people without a place, what is a place without faces, what is a face without a smile and a frown? If tears are the natural counterbalance to laughter and one has to try and laugh as much as she cries to maintain the balance, what is the destiny of those who no longer cry or smile? What am I without a past, presence and a future…without a time and space I call my own, and a soul mate to share time and space with?

Wise men do not fear death. They know that no one can join the realm of the living-dead without death-dancing his way out of the world of the dead living, and that the soul frees itself from the shackles of flesh by breaking free from the manacles of the material and embracing the celestial, supernatural world.

Nobody knew why I decided to take a dive from the earth. Conspiracy theorists suspected foul play. The superstitious blamed witchcraft. Others asserted it was the wrath of the gods and the Supreme One: "To have bad morals is one thing, but having no morals at all is another." "What do you expect of a person who speaks of a homosexual god, a god who is a mother and a father in one-a "he and/or she god?" "That fellow had reached a point where he believed in nothing and a person who believes in no thing is dangerous to himself and to society. Somehow he has to be blotted out of society and the planet."

The psychologically conscious vouched by life that *my excessive love for one woman or another killed me.* Fellow artists put the blame on the frustrations that are the toll of society's pressure upon non-establishment, non-conformist artists and freethinkers. All these suggestions remain but guesswork. I only talked my heart out to the Vaal before I took the ultimate dive. Will they understand the song of the river? Did they recognize me when I came back to life and rediscovered the beauty of human relationship in a woman angel with whom I discovered there is a fruit of life in our loins, but suffered the pain of being the bearer of a miscarried life?

"Esikhathi uvala'zozo
Uphula amawindow
Besingekho mfana
U Botha a tjotja'Mali
Athenga amahippo besingekho
Uzo-joiner Umzabalazo….
Six mabone bra zinga
Vang my sterre
Slaan die vuis
In die Boer se huis."

The sun is down and inmates return from the prison gardens and from other jobs with a song. An aerobic pantomime illustrates a myriad ways of concealing smuggled goods from the hawk-eyed warders, and a variety movements and sounds involved in making sex and faking orgasm. A cacophony of chordless tunes bursts in the air as the Big Fives, Twenty Sixes, Twenty Sevens, Twenty Eighths and the Air Forces collide.   Batons knock sense into a few heads to bring about the silence. A stampede ensues, and dogs are summoned to teach manners to hordes of outlaws. A boot lands on my ribs. The monitor pleads on my behalf.

"That newcomer cannot walk, adjutant. He says police choked his private parts. To me it seems like a drop."
"To hell with him! Who sent him to go and eat rotten cunt? By the way, since when have you become so considerate?"
"No, Boss, I was just…."
"Don't just me! Oh, I see…. You are interested in the bastard because he is fresh from the world and still smells of women. Ha! Ha! HA! Hey, you cow fucker! Go, with this man. He will teach you bedroom manners."
The adjutant rises up a thumb-between-the-fingers sign, and the monitor surveys my buttocks with his hands.
He caresses my thighs and turns towards his master with a green-teeth smile. "Nice, Lekke boude, baas. Baie Dankie"
"Dankie? Ek soek haar lobola! Hundred rands."

Kasie News 2 0ctober 1996

COURT ROUND UP

An eighteen-year old youth charged with the murder of a farmer and his wife was sentenced to fifteen years in jail in the Sasolburg magistrate's court yesterday. Up to the passing of the sentence the youth maintained that he was an innocent passerby who happened to be at the wrong place at the wrong time. He raised the ire of the prosecutor when he claimed that he was just being sacrificed as a token that the police are doing something about the killings of farmers. Delivering judgment judge Koekemoer Sledgehammer pointed out that the court needed to send a strong message to the community that the killing of farmers and other business people will not be tolerated. This incited someone from the court room to shout:" The boy is right. He is a sacrificial lamb."

The court called for silence but the man would not be deterred:" Fucking racists! Who said Apartheid was dead and buried? Apartheid is not dead. It has only been given a face-lift. "The cops grabbed him by his clothes and shoved him out while he ranted unprintable obscenities against the magistrate, giving him the middle-finger.

Meanwhile, SAPA reports that the minister of correctional services says his visits to prisons around the country has assured him that the situation was blown out of proportion by the media and opposition parties. Addressing a press briefing in Sandton, the minister mentioned that hardened criminals and juveniles live in separate cells; as such there were no cases of sodomy. He said it should be taken into consideration that the constitution prevents discrimination against people on the basis of sexual orientation. He added that he personally does not have a problem with homosexuality, as some of his best friends were gay. However, the minister assured the public that condoms are going to be distributed in prisons to combat the spread of HIV/AIDS and other sexually transmitted diseases.

I read the article again and again and muttered to myself:"No sodomy in prisons?" I looked around for a piece of paper to wipe my ass. I did not want to part ways with this particular piece of paper. But I found no other piece. Two inmates came to bring me my food. I heard them talk about me. It is one o'clock and I
hear the music of keys and the rhythm of footsteps.
"What the hell does a newcomer want in the coolkoots?"
"He chewed the monitor's tongue and nearly grilled his private property to mince-meat"
"What do you tune me, gazi? How did that happen?"
"The guluva wanted to mount the boy.
He claimed that the kid was his legal wife, and he paid Adjutant Sheerlust a clipper for his lobola"
The photo of the smiling minister and prison officials glared at me. I read the caption again. **"ALL RIGHT IN PRISONS."**

The scene of the warder selling me for a hundred rands to be another man's wife came to my mind. The words echoed in my ears. "Hey, you cow fucker! Go, with this man.
He will teach you bedroom manners" "Nice, Lekke boude, baas. Baie Dankie"
"Dankie? Ek soek haar lobola! Hundred rands." I took the paper, wiped my ass and flushed, telling myself:
"Next time I go to a tuinspan I will offer an ass-fucking warder free rounds, cut his throat in a moment of drunken ecstasy and run to the free world.
I will embark on a lynch project on farms and place a big billboard on every farm I am through with:
"ALL RIGHT ON THE FARMS."

I was born a rebel, dissenter, and rubble-rouser- the child, who throws tantrums, pisses and raises hell and causes havoc all the time! On my very first day at school the indoctrinators called educators pounced on me and left me with a bleeding ass. My explanation that I was full and the males' loo was fully booked did not suffice as an explanation and plea for mercy. My assertion that all feces are the same was declared as a sign of cheekiness. I spent the next day in hospital. Everyone thought I would return with a much cooler head. But on my return to school I got into trouble again. I decided to piss in the classroom after witnessing one poor lad being clobbered with a broomstick for an improper recitation of the formula for requesting to leave the classroom. I had properly memorized the English and Afrikaans formulations, but the sight of the boy with the bleeding head had terrified me. I feared to confront the crank called "mam" with the request to go to the toilet. I received two punishments that day. The humiliating laughter of pupils who ridiculed me for having a loose bladder and being flogged till the marks made a tree on my back.

An African sage said a wounded bull does not take a revenge on the one that hurt it. I took a brick and crushed the skull of an unlucky lad who saw a bit of shumor in my tragedy and expressed his amusement through laughter.

The day's events reached home before I. Upon arrival, I was bitten to unconsciousness. That Sunday, when everybody slow-motioned their way to the church, I took to the outskirts of the village. I enjoyed dwelling among flowers, speaking to the locusts and making love to the wind. But pain would not leave me. I saw a beehive and the natural inclination for experimentation and probing, call it curiosity and inquisitiveness, moved me to fondle the beehive. The fury of the bees was unleashed. I woke up in hospital, with a swollen head. When I arrived back from hospital, the ogre called principal of the school commanded that I be given countless lashes for my silliness. What did I want in the veld when everybody was in the house of prayer, kneeling before the lord? I wanted to proclaim that I was searching for the maker's face, and to announce the pleasure and ecstasy I derived from mating the locust, the wind and the flowers.

But experience had taught me that some ears are not meant for listening, and that the naked eye cannot see the face and image of God in me.

I learned to take punishment with a smile in my breast and false tears in my eyes. I laughed when they thought I was crying, and cried when they thought I was laughing. Hardly a day passed without me receiving a hiding or a threat that my long ears will be cut and given to the pigs for lunch. I shrugged off the threat as a bluff as I told myself that even the meanest of the two-legged brutes were not capable of such a heinous act. Then I came face to face with the predators called maintainers and keepers of law and order. They pushed hot iron down my ass-hole, dipped my testicles in milk and offered them to the calves to suck. How could I take it as a bluff when the lunatic called special police investigator declared: "I will eat your balls."

I was petrified by the thought of the Dracula munching my balls. Yet I concealed my fear behind a cynical smile. The clown got mad. He landed a punch in my face and a kick on the stomach. I laughed the hyena's laugh. This incited the beast. He came fuming. This time around the whole pack joined in. Fists, boots, gun butts. Batons and death threats. I had learned from previous encounters that it was unwise to show a sign of fear or give any impression that the physical pain somehow touched me psychologically. Any sign of fear or panic would suggest to the vampires that they were on the verge of breaking my spirit. That would delude them into believing that they can buy my conscience with pain.

I was not the one to make their lie appear as truth. My strategy was to unsettle their expectations, and engage them psychologically. If my tormentor kicked the hell out of me, I would be philosophic and ask him the price of his boots. If the lunatic offered me electric shocks, I would request him to pass my regards to his family. If he decided to be persuasive, I would be blunt and ask him to suck my dick. If the torturer opted to threaten me with a jump from the sixth floor, I would be generous and offer to dig his ass or volunteer to mount his wife. So, when the fists, boots and gun butts assailed me, I fell into uncontrollable mirth. The fools stopped abruptly. There was shock in their eyes. They had expected some screaming and a lot of weeping and pleading. The stuff they feed on. That is the stuff that keeps them going.

Breaking bodies and hoping to kill spirits in that process, ignorant of the fact that batons, gun butts, bullets, and machines cannot conquer the human spirit.

I was dragged out of the dungeon with spit on my face and more and more batons caressing my body, taken from a bloody cell to a damn mental asylum. What can a sane man declared insane do to pass the sanity test with flying colors? Perhaps the trick would be to pretend to be insane. The trick resulted in a movement from the asylum to a therapy session.

"Mister… Where shall we begin?" The shrink caressed his goatee." Okay, let us begin with your art." So saying, he pointed to a painting on his table. It was one of the pieces confiscated by the police from my studio on the day that I was arrested for making irreligious and politically incorrect art. In it I had depicted Kuwait as a grinning skull, Saddam's cock in the eye, Bush licking oil oozing from his ass, and Fahad looking on with a sly, half-smile. In the background, in charcoal, I had Saro-Wiwo and his comrades hanging on ropes, and Abacha and the Shell Lords smiling to the bank. I nearly screamed: "How the hell does my work end up here?" I controlled my anger. "This piece is entitled 'Oil is thicker than blood.' Why did you give it that title? Do you consider yourself an impressionist, a surrealist, or a realist? What inspires your art? Do you sometimes put your reflections about the past in your art? I humbly responded: "Sir, you have said such a mouthful that I have already forgotten what you have said. Could you, please repeat the questions?"

"Young man, I've no time for your crazy games! This is no idle game. Right now...."

The fool realized that he had lost his cool. He paused and gave me a half-smile. "My friend, this work of yours is too abstract for me. Tell me, what you are portraying here?"

"Flowers, sir?"

"Young man! I have no time for a circus. I have far better things to do than this interrogation...I mean..."

"I was not aware that I am under interrogation, sir."

"Of course, this is no interrogation. The aim of this therapy session is to help you."

"I think I heard you mention something about interrogation."

"It was a slip of the tongue...hmmm... How do I say it? ... Well, let's talk about your childhood experiences. Your virginity, how did you loose it?" The frog grinned and assumed a business-like posture. I told myself, give the sucker what he wants.

"It all started like this." I began and Mr. Shrink gave me religious attention...a glow of light in his eyes. I whispered inside myself, "Freudian man, let me whet your appetite and leave you salivating - tongue out!"

"Nobody knows the scars within me
There are flowers in my garden
But my house is an island and
My bed is a desert
Nobody knows
The yearning of my heart
Birds are singing up the sky
But nobody knows
The melody of my heartbeat."

The poetry of her movement, the rhythm of her footsteps and the swing of her hips mesmerized eyes. Yet she was single and lonesome. When she was not watering her garden, knitting and sowing or cuddling her pet cat, or reading a magazine, she did other things. But singing is something she did all the time. It was when she danced to the music of her voice that her face lit up like a moon and left me dazzled. I was a little brat then. An inquisitive little boy, who knew not about the loneliness that rocks…the craving and a fervent and burning desire to feel, to be felt, wanted and hungered for. I was starring at her, wondering about the contents of the book in her hands, and thought she was too involved in her reading to notice me.

"Come and read with me"
"I …I…. I cannot read."
"I am not reading…Just watching pictures, come and watch the movie with me."

So saying, she stood up, held my hand and pulled me into her house. We lay on the bed and paged through the rag. My lord! I had never felt like that before. All these years I was never aware that the body could be so wonderful and enthralling. I saw men and women entangled with each other and lost in passion and ecstasy. My body boiled. She called me between her legs or maybe my body volunteered me. I sucked and tucked the magic fruit with the greediness of a calf that has been separated from its mother for a month. She held me tight and moved, danced and hopped like a crazy mule.

She led me out of the room with a childish smile" I hope you now know how to read. My little knight, remember to keep our secret a secret."

I jumped into our yard with a confused mind. Torn apart by the joy of being able to make someone happy and alive and the terrible feeling of feeling unclean and sinful. One part of me celebrated the discovery of how I came to Mother Earth while another cried over the death of innocence. That night I had a string of nightmares. I saw flowers on the breasts of Missus and wine flowing from her pussy. The black bull on top of her, Kleinbaas on top of the bull and my penis joyously ruminating in his ass-hole. The Macula baas came with a rifle, ready to shoot to kill. A bullet in the skull unleashed a scandal on the farm, a talk of the town and a story in the tabloids.

Memory. Time. Space. Place. Period. Context.
Home. Away. Alone. Together. Apart.

Angel. Slut. Love. Lust.

Do words mean anything or are they meant to mean everything, depending on who uses them, when, how, why, where? Is it the words that attach meaning to the actions or is it vice versa? Do words and actions have fixed ever-ready and transcendental meanings or are meanings of words and actions relative, arbitrary and influenced by both subjective and objective reality.

I am digressing. I was telling you about the morning I woke up from the world of slumber to face the harsh and bitter reality that for three full years I've been in love with somebody who was merely whiling away her time with me. No, I was at where I was telling you about my dearly beloved departed baby whose face I long to see but have never known or should I start after my re-memory of the first time I came to know about a loneliness that's like the Nile in the blazing Sahara dessert or before my recollection of the first time I had to die so that I could move on with my life or kill Ashanti and Manyeo in my mind so that I may live? It is when my memory is so fucked up that I find it better to die so that the fictional character can rise up to take this story forward. Remember, for our story to continue the character and the author must die because if they live they will spoil everything by dying, thereby causing our story to die. For the sake of the continuity of our story, the author and the protagonist were long dead before the story began, or the story began long before the narrator and the character were certified dead and reborn.

Remember to re-member that everybody is we because we are because of everybody.
I am everyone and our story takes place wherever everybody is. Every one is part of the story. Every place is the setting of our story. Every time is the period of our story because no matter what / never mind why our story takes place anytime / every time anywhere everywhere, anyhow/ every how. And right now I am dead and I cannot remember whether I was the omniscient narrator or a flat or round character when I died. All I can pray for is that I should be able to reclaim my memory when I come to life again. For now, adios!

TSUNAMI

The area around the court is barricaded with barbed wire and heavily armed policemen are all over. It is quite a struggle for the law enforcers to separate the opposing groups of protestors from each other. On the one side of the fence there is a resonating call, "Justice should be done: Life sentence for Tsunami." On the other side the call is different: "Innocent till proven guilty: Tsunami is a victim of trial by the media." Most people in both camps do not know the real name of the man now popularly and notoriously known as Tsunami nor can they point the man out if they see him walking in the street. All that they have is a picture painted in their minds when they read in the newspapers and hear television and radio reports on the onstage and offstage deeds and misdeeds of Tsunami, the hero turned villain.

You see, in the play of the same name, young girls aged between eighteen and twenty-four years receive telephone calls from a young woman purporting to be calling from a recruitment agency for some secretarial companies that are affirmative action and equity employers. She/he then sets up an appointment with the girls and meets them at the designated spot. From there she/he takes them to the outskirts of the township where she/he claims that the car from the employment agency will pick them up. Days thereafter the girls are found raped and dead, with one lacerated breast and a grotesquely huge T-shaped wound on the other.

The serial killer character wears a wig and thick lipstick that gives him/her a Naomi Campbell look, and she/he has the same shapes. *(?) Her movements are convincing and so is the voice. The audience never gets to see the face, as the actual rape and murder scenes are not portrayed in the play. All that the audience hears are hysterical and anguished screams and mad groans, gruesome writhing and the gnashing of teeth. Thereafter they see tattered clothes and floods of blood and hear the gruesome details of the murder as explained by other characters in the play. As the events in the play took place at the time of the news of the tsunami disaster in Asia and some parts of Africa, the other characters in the play referred to the serial killer character as Tsunami.

The real-life re-play of the "Tsunami serial rape-killings" took place three months after the tsunami disaster. By that time, the play has been previewed to quite a few audiences at various places in the Vaal Triangle Area. Within the group the name Tsunami had come to be associated with the fiery and fearsome character as well as the public-shy actor who portrayed him so well. Then our group was hit by a Tsunami. It started with the girl who performs the part of the woman who kills Tsunami in the play receiving a call from a young lady purporting to be a theatre director. She claimed that she had seen our member in performance and was keen to include her in her cast that was about to go to Germany on a cultural exchange program. They set up an appointment to meet each other at the outskirt of Zamdela, near the Sasol industrial area from where they would drive to Johannesburg for the auditions.

That was the last time she was seen alive. Her body was found a week latter in the same conditions as the victims of Tsunami. As we were still trying to make sense of the story, a young girl and a teenage boy who were part of our cast were found in similar conditions. And then it was three young high school girls and one teenage boy.

People were shocked. Some suspected that they were victims of "Mzekezeke", a serial rapist who lured his victims with promises of jobs and was caught red-handed in a balaclava while raping a kid he had duped into believing that he was the hooded Kwaito star whose stage-name is Mzekezeke. They speculated that "Mzekezeke" was enraged that Tsunami was actually a disguised take off on him. But it turned out that 'Mzekezeke' was in jail at the time Tsunami struck.

Township gossip had it that the fellow in prison was the wrong guy. The said the DNA test had revealed that his semen does not match with that found in the girl who was raped. The story was that the real "Mzekezeke" was outside and he was the one responsible for the Tsunami rape-killings. But then the original "Mzekezeke" never raped males. Others suggested that there were a number of serial rapists and killers taking advantage of the "Mzekezeke/Tsunami saga." At the end of the day, "Mzekezeke" was no longer talked about. Tsunami had taken over.

True to the tradition of "the show must go on", we at the Biko Community Theater Project continued with our Tsunami project, staging benefit shows for the victims of the other tsunami- HIV/AIDS. Then one day the police came to our rehearsal room and arrested Tsunami. Some of the cast members tried to obstruct the police, while others just shook their heads in disbelief and a few actually murmured that they have been silently wondering whether Tsunami is indeed the Tsunami. I intervened and pleaded with the group members to let the police do their job and wait for the court decision before they allow the issue to divide the group or to put us at odds with the law and community.

Now I stand in the middle of the two opposing and protesting camps. Belonging to none and still confused as to what to believe and what not to. But I am one of the few people who know the young man and the face that now bear the name Tsunami. Actually I am the one who created the character called Tsunami and her namesake, Tsunami the play. I should rather say I am the one who planted the seeds because I only came up with the concept and facilitated the experimental workshopping of the play collectively by the group and allowed each character to explore various ways of developing his or her character.

From the beginning I was fascinated by the passion with which our man launched into the project of constructing and developing his character. He went to all court proceedings where there was a murder or rape case, kept press clippings of stories on serial killers, took tons upon tons of documents off the internet and watched every movie he could get on the subject of serial killers and serial rapists.
He interviewed police and psychologists who are experts on serial killers and also talked to friends and relatives of the serial killers. His idea was that to be able to portray a character, in this case a serial killer, you do not just have to understand his background and his psychology, but have to also get into his boots, share his dreams and nightmares, fantasies and fears and hopes, wrap yourself in his mind and soul and see the world from his point of view. That he managed to do that is beyond doubt.

This naturally humble and cool and collected youngster became a bloodthirsty monster on stage. The fire in his eyes and the rage in his voice as well as the physical force with which he expressed it, scared even fellow actors and left the audiences spellbound by the beast that man is capable of becoming. He excelled in the court scene, where he related the story of Tsunami, how he was born to an eighteen-year-old girl who abandoned him for the life of pleasure and left him in the care of her blind and aged granny, how his ex-convict uncle used to sodomize him and how he was once gang-raped by a group of older girls after they found him doing to their sibling what his uncle used to do to him.

Overnight he became the hero of the township theater scene. Everyone wished they could see the actor playing the Tsunami character. But he made sure that after every performance he went offstage to join the other crew of the Biko Community Theatre Project. Off course, offstage Tsunami was always a closed book. He was quiet and self-effacing and seldom spoke about himself or his family and childhood.

As a hairdresser and cross-dresser, he was most of the time in the company of girls, and was what the Mzansi ladies refer to as "a dish" (or "a gorgeous piece of meat," as Queen Moroka of Generations would put it). Yet he shied away from romantic relations with girls. One would have easily assumed he was homosexual, if he did not display such an antagonistic attitude towards gays, and verbally abused those who mistakenly tried to charm their way into his life. He openly declared that one thing he agreed with Mutable about was the fact that gays and lesbians are worse than baboons. That was about all that we the members of group knew and could tell the police and the court about our colleague.

We were all shocked to hear the story related by his mentally deranged granny in court that he was actually a victim of sexual molestation when he was a child. She claimed that Tsunami's mother gave birth to him at the tender age of fourteen and died in the process and that his aunt and legal guardian used him as a sex slave, as her husband had become sexually impotent after being confined to a wheelchair by a car accident. But how reliable can the evidence of an insane old woman be? As much as Tsunami was an enigma to us in the group, it is much more difficult to find another actor who will get into the boots of the Tsunami character the way he did. Or shall we not proceed with the play?

DJ YOGHURT

"Be cautious and careful my child, Gauteng is not a safe place. If a month passes without finding him, come back. Don't stay for too long there. That place turns human beings into strange creatures. Go well my child, may God be with you."

Chapel is not concentrating on the old woman's parting words as he painfully reflects on the contents of the letter his mother received from his father ten years ago: "I was forced to marry you because you got pregnant after the fling I was forced to have with you to prove that I am a man but now I have found myself and I am not prepared to come back because I cannot afford to live the life of pretence anymore. Goodbye. God bless you and the child."

The journey by taxi from Maseru to Johannesburg is a very tiring one, but the music on the radio and conversation it sparks among the passengers provides comic relief for Chakela. The hot subject is a specific song by his namesake, Chakela- the musician who has recently taken the music scene in Lesotho by storm. This particular song has lyrics with metaphoric reference to love affairs and sexual relationships between men and young girls and between young men and older women. In the song the singer seem to be condoning these kinds of relationships by indicating that it is quite natural and logical for older men to have a liking for mabolotsane -pumpkin in its early stage of growth- as it is much softer for their teeth, and for young boys to eat pumpkin as they have sharper teeth. The taxi driver joins in the conversation, arguing that it is irresponsible for a musician to use such a powerful tool of communication as music to encourage things that are out of touch with the norms and values of society.

The young man sitting next to Chakela throws in his own idioms in support of the musician. "Chakela o opile kgomo ka lenaka, ntate. Kgomo di hangwa ke bashanyana" Chakela is surprised to hear his feminine voice and his strange accent. He also notices he has womanish mannerism in the way he gestures and shakes his head when he talks. He had observed this effeminate movement when the fellow boarded the taxi but did not take it seriously.

A woman in tight jeans and a "stomach-out" body suit, whose wrinkled face betrays the fact that she is not as young as her body and dress and mannerism suggests, enters the conversation in support of the young man. She responds that culture is not static, it moves with the times. She adds that age has got nothing to do with love and one's feelings but what is important is how the couple feels about each other and what brings happiness into one's life.

The older woman seated next to her retorts: "Don't talk about love and feelings and happiness. All that these men are interested is our bodies and to satisfy their insatiable appetite for sex not anything else. After the old man has used your body he returns to his wife and children and leaves you with a fatherless child. The same happens with these young boys, they have sexual affairs with the older people but continue to maintain love relationships with younger girls. As for these women who sleep with boys, they are a disgrace to themselves and to their children. Imagine sharing a boyfriend with your daughter. What happens when your son discovers that his friend is your girlfriend? Sies! Ke manyala kaofela nthwena" The wrinkled faced woman quips. "I am more interested in emotional and sexual satisfaction than in moralistic judgments. These old men tire in less than three minutes. What should I be doing all the time he snores? Painting my nails throughout the night?'

Once again the young man who speaks Sesotho with an Anglo-American accent resorts to the language of metaphors to argue his case: "O nepile wena, Mme. Pitsa e sokwa ka lesokwana. Lebekere le foduwa ka tea spoon" The taxi driver shakes his head and look at the young man with disdain written all over his face: ."Look at this man-woman, or are you woman-man? What do you know about love affairs between real men and real women?" He turns towards Chakela: "It is true what your old woman told you. Do not stay in Jo'burg for too long, my son. You will come back home without your identity, knowing little of Sesotho and mastering English more than the Queen – a strange creature neither black nor white, and neither male or female."

The young man is not gagged by the taxi driver's tirade. Shaking his head and pulling back his long hair from his face with one hand as he gestures with the other, he bursts out: "You Basotho are backward. You are still caged in the dark ages and you want everybody to conform and be trapped in the chains of social control. I choose to be what I feel. I am and who I choose to be. That's why I have decided to live in Jo'burg. Jozi allows you to be who you are."

As the music gives way to the news and current affairs, conversation changes to political issues. Not impressed by political discussion or maybe avoiding further confrontation with the taxi driver, the young fellow turns to Chakela and softly engages him in a conversation. His name is Yoghurt and he is a model, singer and dancer and also works as a DJ in a club owned by a friend of the man he is in love with, but his final dream is to spin the discs at YFM and release his own CD of a fusion of house and kwaito, which he plans to call Kwai-House.

Chakela suppresses his shock. He had thought the fellow only had feminine looks, but here he is confirming the fact that he is gay. As the conversation goes Chakela also opens up and tell the man his story. His mother passed away two weeks ago and his sick grandmother feels that she's about to leave planet earth too. She has therefore requested him to go and look for his father who disappeared into South Africa ten years ago, when he was only fourteen years old.

A guy from Maseru who recently returned from Johannesburg after he was confined to a wheel chair by a car accident has told the family that he heard from friends that Chakela's father runs some business in Johannesburg at a place called Yeoville. But the only relatives whose contact numbers he has are in Embalehle in Secunda. Since the taxi will arrive late in Johannesburg he does not even know where to stay for the night. Maybe he will sleep at the taxi rank.

The young man tells him that he stays in Yeoville but unfortunately there will be no accommodation for Chakela at his boyfriend's one-room flat. And he also does not want to make him jealous by arriving with another man. Otherwise he knows Yeoville like he knows himself and will be willing to help him find his father. He gives him his cellular phone numbers.

The jean-clad woman has been eavesdropping on the conversation. As soon as they disembark from the taxi she approaches the two young men and introduces herself as Clara. She tells them that she works and stays in Hillbrow, not far from Yeoville and can offer Chakela accommodation for the night. Yoghurt bids them goodbye and says he will wait for their call tomorrow. Clara is first to break the ice. She tells Chakela she is working at a clothing shop in Central Johannesburg and stays at a flat in Hillbrow. She asks about his father.

Chakela relates that his father's name is Josefa Masemola. He worked as a bus driver in Lesotho and is alleged to have started off as a taxi driver in Vereeniging and later went to Johannesburg were he is reported to be having some business. They take a maxi taxi to the flat.

The following day Chakela wakes up in a confused state. He had never imagined himself between the legs of a woman old enough to be his mother and whispering a love song in her ears. Clara asks him what size he wears and tells him to feel at home and relax for the day while she will be at work. . She comes back with designer clothes and flashy shoes for him. She takes out a box of KFC and they eat. Thereafter they bath and change clothes. Chakela looks like a street wise, man-about-town, Jo'burg clever in his new outfit. They call their gay friend for directions to the club and Clara tells Chakela to relax in the bedroom for the day as she goes about her chores. At six o'clock in the evening they take a cab to Joe's Club in Yeoville. On arrival they are welcomed by the happy Yoghurt who introduces them to his boyfriend, "Joseph Messemla."

GUMBA

"The subscriber is not available at the moment try again later"

…the voice tells me and to no avail I try again later several times until I decide to try the guys' home phones and I am met with voice mails or phones ringing endlessly without anyone picking them up and I hopelessly shake my head, painfully trying to understand how it is possible that it could be but just a coincidence that all the guys have either switched their phones off or have left them home or lost them and now I am wondering whether these guys are still coming because they were so adamant that our New Year's Eve get-together should take place at Mafeshene's place in Houghton despite the fact that last year we were at the very same place and the years before that we had it at Majivane's joint in Midrand and at Mafesha's mansion in Reigerpark. I asked them what is wrong with my house and they all chorused: "Will there be security for our cars." Their girls added their own verses: "There's sure to be gate-crushers and we won't be able to wear our jewelry." They ended their song on a high note: "We've been telling you for too long that that place is a security risk and any businessman worth his salt should have long considered trekking."

To say I was gatvol is an understatement as I do not understand how can anyone have the guts to express such a negative generalization about the place I love so much and to boot how is it possible that this hellish depiction of my hometown comes from the very homeboys and girls I grew up and played games with in the dusty streets. Are these not the same people with whom I share sweet and loving memories of get-downing all night long kuzekuse on countless lala-vuka occasions and with whom I patrolled the streets to protect the community from attacks by Otheliweni Imidlwembe Ama-Askari and other faceless ruthless manifestations of the third force. Did we not together wipe various marauding gangs from the streets of our hometown? Was Mafeshene not the feared commander of the defense units before he exchanged the khaki trousers with those made- in –Paris- for- the -select -monied –few designer suits and was Mafesha not himself a courier for drug lords before we gave him morabulo and won him to the side of Umzabalazo and long before he became notorious for laying down she-comrades with sweet talk and sheer brute force at times? Did we not dance the dark streets together and what is the difference between these streets these days and these streets those days? For sure there were muggings, jack rolling and hijacking then as is the case today and of course like it is today that was not all there was here. There was fighting and loving and fucking and partying and dying and burying and hoping and praying and building then as is the case now.

Clearly it is them and not the streets that have changed. Indeed they have changed or else how do you explain the fact that they have decided to change their minds at the eleventh hour and decide not to come despite the fact that I finally had managed to force them to accept the fact that it is my turn to host the gumba and that since I choose to stay here this where the gig will be? Perhaps it is too early for me to jump to conclusions, after all it is only nine o'clock and we said the mimic will start at half past seven so this might just be a case of sticking to African time. All I can say at the moment is I hope/ I wish/perhaps/maybe/supposing/what if/

"The subscriber is not available at present try again later"

Says the voice but this is the umpteenth time that I am trying to get hold of Minivan and it is the same story with Mafesha and Mafeshene and their ladies. Every time I call each one of them the voice declares "you have reached the cell phone of... and when I try again later it looks as if the lady has gone tired from blurting out one story a million times because this time around I just hear some inaudible gibberish hush-hushing and ending off with:

"At the tone please leave a message or hang up".

These are guys who simply would not let their batteries go flat for such a long time and they certainly know how to handle their cells with tender loving care and not let them fall down since they do not go around with some cheap-cheap fong kong mokokotelo from some back-door operation but with brand new genuine makoya designer things fresh and straight from the store. Hence I wonder what happened to their cells and shudder to think what could have happened to them because their grinning skulls would haunt me in my every waking and sleeping moment to tell me they told me that only people with death wishes dare to drive around with expensive cars in the night in Soweto of all places and in Zola nogal.

I was indeed offended when they asked me when will I see the light that nothing can be as dangerous as darkies who can make a deal with your car while you are still driving around in it or dare to sell your flashy shoes while your are still strutting about wearing them and do not mind taking a human life for a cell phone they will exchange for a case of beer or for a BM series 1 that they will trade in for one thousand five hundred rands. I blasted out that I was born and shall die in Zola and am no chicken feed to be hoodwinked into joining the chicken flight and therefore contributing to the brain-drain in the ghetto simply because some brain-twisted westoxicated and white-washed darkies who climbed up the corporate ladder on the bee & aa bandwagon are now depicting the very place that gave them the breath of life as some hell on earth that is worse than Sodom and Gomorrah to justify their transformation into social hermits who find succor in the concrete jungle and hide from each other behind the safety of barbed wire and the security of armed guards and alarm systems.

Now I am exhausted from waiting and waiting and am also bloody tired of hearing;

"You've reached/
 the voicemail of/
  the subscriber is not available
   at the tone
    try again later..."

I open a bottle of vodka and start drinking to keep myself busy while waiting for the guys and curse myself for relying on them to pick Beauty up at her home on their way to my place. Now I am alone and efforts to reach her on her cell are also in vain. I try her younger sister's cell but the phone cuts while she's busy trying to tell me that Beauty left her home two hours ago. Damn the fucking phone to cut just when I am about to seek clarity leaving me with non-conclusive clues to what could possibly have happened or be happening. I do not know when and how sleep overcame me but I wake up at 9 am with red eyes and a bloody raving headache supplemented by a rebelling tummy and so I down a regmaker and Eno at the same time as I once again start asking myself question after question sparking more questions without answers until I give in and stop trying to rationalize and interrogate what could have happened and resort to phoning again….

"You've reached

the voicemail of…

at the tone please

leave a message

or hang up

the subscriber

is not available

at the moment

at the tone ------ ".

News bulletin:…. a white red Caravel Kombi collided with a truck on the N1 road last night at about eight o'clock. The only surviving passenger in the Caravella told SABC news from a hospital bed that they were heading to a party in Soweto. Witnesses claim that the driver was on his mobile phone when….

Bliksem!

THE PROPHECY

17 August 2000

The picture of the young man from Eldorado Park shot dead at the gate of a house in Westdene is in the front pages of the newspapers. Many in the black community are enraged. They cry that Black life remains cheap in the new South Africa, as white people frequently get acquitted or receive lenient sentences for killing black people for trivialities such as trespassing or a farm worker's dog mating with a farmer's dog, while Black people often receive long sentences for crimes such as cattle theft and housebreaking.

"What about the farmers daily killed in their houses and a lot of us who are victims of car hijacking and house breaking? Many people have been killed in these incidents of car hijacking and burglary without the law bringing the perpetrators to book. What are we supposed to do", asks Jaap Koekemoer rhetorically, "should we smile and dance while we are being lynched?"

Kobus shakes his head and gives his uncle a half-smile, "Lynch is a heavy word, Oom. I am sure most of the cases result from pure acts of desperateness by people driven to stealing and other criminal activities by sheer hopelessness in the face of rampant poverty and squalor. And these are isolated acts of criminality, rather than concerted and collective acts of violence against the farmers or white people."

Elise has been listening to the two men's' conversation with her eyes focused on the newspaper. "Die een lyk net soos n' Boer vir my. Ek het nie n' boesman wat so lyk gesien in my lewe" At this remark both men turn their attention to the young man's photo. "Rerig, hy lyk net soos Oom. Jy kan sweer sy's Jaap Koekemoer Junior."

Elise and Kobus's laughter is interrupted by Oom Paul's angry outburst, accusing Kobus of insulting him for likening him with a stinking dead hotnot. Holding him by the scruff of the neck, Oom Paul tells Kobus that while he can tolerate the fact that his nephew is a politically correct kaffir-boetie, he cannot stand him challenging the purity of his Afrikaner blood. He bursts out of the room, shouting obscenities. Kobus is frightened, "I better fly out of here. The old man is going to kill me."

But Elise is still in her humorous vein: "Hold it, Kobus just check the coincidence. This guy's name is Japie Koekies De Bruin. This is one of our long lost relatives, ek se; I just wonder how he landed in Eldoradopark."

14 February 1985

The fire in the eyes of the youths spoke an unexpressed rage as they fell into a crazy aerobic dance, chanting angry songs about Botha's wife giving birth to rats and Tambo's conceiving freedom soldiers, and denouncing the tricameral system as a shamocracy. The more and more the police tried to hold them back, the more and more the marchers stormed forward in rage. The colonel shouted instructions to the crowd to disperse in five minutes and threatened that failure to do so will result in the police taking tough action.

Sergeant Koekemoer felt a sense of déjà vu. He has witnessed a similar march ending in chaos. Three hundred youths shot dead and four policemen badly injured, one dying later in hospital. Later the police claimed that they shot in self-defence as stones and petrol bombs were thrown at them, but the comrades claimed that the police shot peaceful marchers unprovoked.

As he was busy re-winding this scene in his mind and anticipating a replay, Koekemoer heard a loud voice instructing the marchers to stay calm and hold back. To his surprise the huge mass obeyed the commander as if it was a choir hearkening to the instruction of the choirmaster. Five leaders of the protest led by a tall, slender phony-looking youngster stepped forward. In a calm and sober voice, the boy requested the colonel to give the crowd at least twenty to thirty minutes to disperse, as it was difficult for such a huge crowd to disperse in five minutes. The colonel shouted obscenities, threatening the young leader with arrest. The people responded with anger, some surging forward and others accusing their leadership of leniency and cowardice. But the youngster calmly told the crowd that it is a well-known ploy of the police to rouse peaceful protestors into desperate action so that they may justify their acts of brutality. He asked the people not to provide the police with a justification for shooting at them, and turned to the Colonel to further plead with him to give the crowd more time to disperse.

As the Colonel gave out new instructions, giving the protestors thirty minutes to disperse, Koekemoer wondered to himself where he has seen the youngster before. He felt sure that the big and bright eyes and the soft but articulate voice belonged to someone he knew. He got the strange idea that the boy was actually a woman in a man's body. Suddenly the image came to him. Maria - soft but outspoken, castigating him for allowing his individuality to be swallowed up by the bigger noise of society and accusing him of not eating the guinea fowl but devouring the gravy thereof - a reference to the fact that he served and supported the racist policies of the Apartheid state but had secret romantic and sexual affairs with Black people. Koekemoer took some time to look at the boy and felt the urge to launch himself at him, tear his clothes apart and wrap himself around the gorgeous female body that he was very sure was hidden behind the angry face of the young revolutionary, clad in tattered jeans and a Steve Biko T-shirt.

27 August 2000

The Eldorado Park man killed in Westdene last week was a photo-journalist busy with a photo-documentary on his family history as a way of capturing the tragedy of children who were products of sex across the colour line under apartheid.

In 1967 Maria De Bruin entered into a secret affair with a white policeman who was stationed at Westbury Police station where she worked as a cleaner. A year later she got pregnant with his child.

After getting bits and bits of information from the diary of his mother, and through interviews with some people - including police who worked at the Westbury Station in the 80's, Japie Koekies De Bruin went to Westdene to try and get an interview with a retired policeman, Jaap Marais Koekemoer - the man who allegedly fathered him.

He mistakenly went to the house of Jan Skieter, Koekermoer's neighbour, whose house was broken into the week before. Still embittered by the incident, Skieter shot Japie dead. He claims that Japie carried something that looked like a gun, and was pointing it at him when he decided to shoot him.

Kobus read the newspapers several times and pinched himself to assure himself that he was not a daydreamer. How is Aunt Elise going to take the news? He recalled her humorous prophetic statement: "This is one of our long lost relatives..."

COMRADE RED SOCKS

07 November 2005
The secretary
Revolutionary Democratic Party for a Mixed Economy
1994 Adam Smith Avenue
1ˢᵗ Floor Karl Marx Building
Sandton

Dear Sir

My apologies, comrade Gen Sec, pardon the occasional slip of the tongue, I have just returned from the meeting of the board of trustees of Amandla Investments. Surely you will understand the switch from official lexicon to revolutionary language may not be that easy, after heated discussions on how to reconcile our move towards offshore investments in the face of stiff and tight competition with the ideal of patriotic and responsible corporate practices. I must tell you guys, the real revolution is in the boardroom; to negotiate for a place and define one's identity in the boundary space between the realities of dialectics and the imperatives of the market is no mean feat.

For my very first corporate meeting, I really did not know what to wear. Habitually I went for my vintage Che Guevara style red-star beret, my hammer and sickle Soviet T-shirt, old bang-bang jeans and a pair of takkies and my trademark red socks. But then I thought about offending some of my partners. By then the Madiba shirt was not yet a fashion craze, and there were only three suits in my wardrobe. I do not want to even mention the one I wore for my graduation ceremony. It reminds me of my most embarrassing days when I snubbed the popular boycott of graduation ceremonies at Mangosuthu Tech and bowed to Gatsha Buthelezi to get my cap. The one I adorned on my wedding day is rather too grayish and boringly English. Though the faded colour and the size betrayed that it was an inheritance, the collar-neck "Nehru suit" I inherited from my late father was just the right choice.

Anyway I am digressing; I hereby wish to apologize for not attending last night's consultation without tendering an apology. I was just about to do so when I got an urgent invitation to dine with the minister of trade and industry from the Democratic Republic of Taiwan. Of course, I know party matters are very important, but I know you will agree that to protect Black Economic Empowerment is a crucial side of the second phase of the revolution... It is important for vigilant cadres like yours truly to be present at all occasions of this nature. I understand that the consultation has been rescheduled to next Monday and I would have loved to attend but as you know, ever since I was deployed from the labor to the government sector, half of my day is spent in meetings; breakfast with analysts, lunch with the chairman, dinners to clinch deals & Summit TV to keep posted on the goings on in the business scene. A quarter is consumed by golf and fishing for business contacts. Another is taken up by networking-cum-socializing, quality time with my wife and (off the record) fantasizing about me between my personal assistant's legs.

Wishing you success in your deliberations

Yours in the national democratic revolution

Comrade Red Socks

THE RECONFIGURATION OF COMRADE SLOGAN

Part 1

Headline news: "DOYEN OF PEOPLE'S THEATRE COMMITS SUICIDE."
He threw himself from the fourteenth floor of a dingy flat in Hillbrow. He was squatting with an actor friend lucky enough to put a piece of bread on the table by appearing in some television sitcom cautioning people against illegal reconnections of water and electricity, land invasion and other such acts of hooliganism.
. The story is accompanied by pictures of him flying his way to death and of his body lying dead and cold on the dead and cold concrete pavement. They are juxtaposed against photos of him doing the toi-toi at the ceremony to welcome the returnee exiles at FNB Stadium in 1990... performing an outstanding piece on the Sharpeville shooting...conducting a people's theatre workshop. Obituaries wax lyrical about how patriotic he was and how he selflessly gave limb and body, mind and soul to the freedom struggle. A group of artists are digging into their pockets to raise money for his funeral and a trust fund has been set up. There are talks of putting out a publication featuring his works of visual art, a collection of his plays, essays and short stories and a photo-album on his stage performances. Some people are suggesting that his works should be in the curriculum at all government schools. A fellow artist commits himself to putting on a dance-drama-cum-opera on his life, off and on-stage. Some big company is ready to fork out the big bucks.

I stare in wonder thinking about our last encounter. He came in the office with a face with anxiety written all over it, his anger passionately refusing to be suppressed. I have to intervene, he said. He has put all his life in this script. It is beyond narrow definitions and categorizations of artistic expression. In it there is poetry, song, movement, mime, story- telling, drama, sermonizing, lecturing, pain, joy, celebration, mourning and everything that is part of human experience. The actors and singers and dancers and storytellers and preachers and lecturers and activists are all masters in their fields. Three years of brainstorming and rehearsals – improvisations and innovations-have gone into it. People who are clued-up on the subject matter and very passionate about the message have done more than enough research. But funding is simply not coming to put the work on stage. None of the theatres around is prepared to even include the project in their developmental projects.

He has also tried to start small and stage the work in small community halls and in schools and churches. But nobody wants to have anything to do with the project. Close comrades he literally spent entire lifetimes with- serving in the street committees, doing people's theatre and sacrificing in the defence committees, not to mention suffering underground and doing time in apartheid jails- have accused him of being a struggle romantic. They say he's been sleeping through the revolution.

Who is interested in a play about the small people who fanned the fires of resistance through experimental theatre and street theatre? For a realist, what happened to the guy who used to do tap dance in the streets of Johannesburg (I can remember the name, I think it was Joe something) is not a priority. Who cares to know who composed "Nantsi Mellow-Yellow" or who was the greatest toi-toi dancer in and around the PWV area in the 80's at the time such an area is not even on the map of South Africa? Why not move with the song of Umfolozi, dance the protea and the springbok…rhyme to the beauty of the green valleys and smiling hills, compose an anthem for 2010? And hip to the re-birth of Eugene Terreblanche or think something creative over a braai vleis, over Whisky & Jack D over the sounds of Mafikizolo on a sunny Sunday morning?

His own father has accused him of being a hero of yesterday, in search of a cause to pursue today, because he performs at the gatherings of the Treatment Action Campaign, the Landless People's Movement and the Anti-Privatization Movement. The old man said frustration at not being in the top echelon of the party, let alone making it to local government, has made him hang around good-for-nothing ultra-radicals suffering from anti-everything-ism.

"All your friends are in parliament. That boy next door was a police spy in the struggle years but he is a favorite to be the mayor. Your brother has been re-deployed to the corporate sector. Just now you will call him a fat cat. He has betrayed labour and has embraced capital. But what can you boast of? …A great toi-toi dancer turned performing artist. Listen to me, my boy. This grey hair is a mark of wisdom, I have been in both Poqo and Umkhonto and most importantly, I fathered, raised you and gave you a political education…. All this nostalgic talk about telling the story of people's culture through new forms of artistic expression is bullshit. And the whole nonsense about combating the tyranny of capital is daydreaming. Everybody has embraced the supremacy of the market in the Global Village. All the struggle heroes have done so. Even your big friend Gaddafi has embraced real politics and befriended the West to court global capital. Castro will follow suit in a matter of time or he will eat dust and rust in the dustbins of history like Saddam.

"Who do you think you are? After all you were never anything but a sloganeering idiot who graduated into a glorified "Comrade Slogan"- a people's poet. But poetry for a cause is a dead horse, man. Stop looking for accolades for being the great singer of freedom songs and wake-up to the post-freedom songs, my man: embrace poetry for beauty's sake and dance to the poetics of Capital."

In defence he told the old man "I am just an artist giving expression to the voice of the people and articulating their fears and hopes, dreams and aspirations." To his surprise his young communist brother, who had just landed himself a job as Executive Director at Thari E Ntsho Investments, exploded: "That's bullshit, big brother! How can you call supporting people, who see no good but wrongdoing in the Government of the People, as giving the people a voice? Papa is right; you are a good man in search of a cause."

That hurt him more than the sword of Brutus piercing Caesar's heart. Perhaps that's the real reason why his younger brother asked him to move out of his house, using the complaints of his wife as an excuse. Not only has he become a burden and embarrassment to his family for being uncircumcised, unemployed, unmarried and homeless at the age of forty. He has become somebody they have to disown in order to keep the family name in the good books of the powers that be.

Now he's come to me, his childhood friend and longtime comrade-in-arms. He is sceptical about everybody in the corridors of power and calls them "former guerrillas turned gorillas feeding on instead of feeding the poor." But he has somewhat retained his confidence in me. We have always shared a passion for theatre and the arts and the belief in culture as a weapon of the people. My baritone voice always complemented his mellow tenor whenever freedom songs were sung.

I vividly remember one morning at the hideout. He woke up in excitement. He had dreamt of us ambushing a mellow-yellow. After the job was done he stood on top of a rock and sang a song celebrating our fearlessness in the face of the system's sophisticated weaponry. We sat and worked on the song while other comrades tucked in on morabulo, going to town about what Marx meant by the withering away of the state. He struggled to remember the words but finally we put some lyrics together. I came up with the tune. We sang at the top of our voices and the comrades stopped everything they were doing and joined us. The song became an instant hit. To this day various versions of the song can be heard sung at students' meetings, workers' gatherings and at congresses of various organizations that were part of the liberation movement.

How can I forget these sweet moments? How can he not trust in me? I'm the one who launched into our defence when ideologues and combatants belittled us and called us "Bo-Comrade Slogan" or accused us of fiddling while Rome burns. "It is the sound of the bazooka and not free verses that shall make the land to be shared amongst those who live in it… for the people to share in the country's wealth…for the doors of learning and culture to be opened…for peace, security, comfort to reign…. for food to be plenty that no one may be hungry." I argued that every struggle needs a bard, and that culture is a site of struggle. I said music is the healer and our poetry is the voice of the voiceless.

That even in post-apartheid South Africa there will be a need to give artistic and cultural expression to the socio-economic and political realities facing the people. That when freedom dawns there would be fresh matters to address and new issues to hype about and hip to. That people will still be people and they will still need a song and a dance to express their sorrows and frustrations. That our role would be to compose new songs and inspire people toconfront the issues of the day and consolidate the gains made by the people on the terrain of the struggle. I said the bard's role would be to be a watchdog against revisionism and counter-revolution. My argumentation moved some high-ranking party officials to lobby against the party's decision to close its cultural wing on the eve of liberation.

But today I am in a completely different position. As the Director of the Department of Arts and Culture in the local government I have been part of the decision to privatize some of the public theatres, stadiums and other sporting and cultural amenities. I am also in the process of courting private capital to sponsor the few of the public theatres and arts and culture centres that have escaped privatization. There is nothing I can do and nothing much I can say. I am just implementing government policy. I have a job to take care of.

After all, over the years I have become convinced that if we leave the economy on its own, it will take care of itself and everything shall follow. That in the initial phase the economic growth yielded by liberalization and state withdrawal shall benefit only a tiny and minute, propertied and learned few. But in the long run the benefits will slowly but surely trickle down to the masses on the ground. As much as I have very fond memories of our times in people's theatre, I simply believe that its time is over. But how do I tell my friend? How do I tell him that his script makes ideological but not economic sense?

I am afraid that being seen endorsing his script might cause me to be added to the list of ultra-radical leftists, and therefore jeopardize my position. I offered to think about the issue and kept skirting around it every time he came to see me. To ease my conscience, I regularly offered to take him out on a drinking spree and gave him some money. I also shared all the freebies I get on account of my position in society with him. I have become so stupid; I never noticed that this irritates him.

One day he gave me a piece of his mind: "Listen comrade, I am not here as a beggar, but as an artist who needs nothing but to be given a chance to showcase his talent and make a contribution to the country. Why don't you simply face up to the truth and tell me that you too believe that the market must dictate which productions get sponsored and which should receive publicity and a platform?"

I was left speechless. I was still thinking of words to philosophize and euphemize the issue when he stormed out of my office. His facial expression and body movements said it all. "I shall never set foot in your office again." Now I look at his picture and hopelessly try to suppress my tears. I imagine him barking at me, commanding me not to cry for him. The phone rings. It is a request for me to speak at his memorial service.

To prepare for the speech I go through his works. I just cannot avoid returning to the script on people's theatre, so powerfully loaded with striking images of struggle and survival, witty and sarcastic humour and brilliant portrayals of the resilience of the human spirit. I am hooked on the scene portraying the internal and external struggles of one of the many blind people who can be seen on the streets of the cities of South Africa and the world…. Singing their hearts out to a world keen on hearing but not listening to the call in their music.

> "Ha ke hloke kutlwelo-bohloko
> Ke hloka ho utwlisiswa
> Se ka ntjheba, ntsebe
> Se ka nkutlwella, nkutlwe."

He sits in a corner nearby Park Station and plays his flute all day long. The melody is something that could rock Mozart from the dead out of the grave on to the dance floor. A reckless taxi driver nearly hits him. Passers-by and onlookers jeer at the driver, who in turn, calls their mothers all sorts of names. Someone throws some coins in the tin and hurries to wherever his feet are taking him to. Another throws in a note. A few are moving and jiving to the music. Others just give sympathetic looks. Slowly, poignantly, choreographic, he shuffles and whispers a tune, so soft that to most people it is a wordless hum:

> *"When you are up and I am down*
> *Forget not to remember*
> *All that goes up must come down*
> *When everybody is up and you rise up*
> *Remember not to forget*
> *All that goes up must converge."*

The sun is just about to go down and he is now on a completely wordless tune. But my friend with his spiritual ear can hear in the song the yearning of the blind musician for the people to appreciate his music for its quality, rather than simply fork out coins and notes out of sympathy, without even caring to take heed of the stylistic and thematic content of the music. Yes, says my friend, the song does have lyrics but because people choose not to bother to listen, they will never hear the words and their message. He says the song says something about the frustration of the man at being heard rather than listened to, and being patronized because he is blind instead of being acknowledged as a terrifically talented artist.

> *"The point is not the sight but the insight*
> *My music is not for the hearing but for the listening*
> *I need no sympathy but understanding."*

Part 2

I will be smiling all the way to the bank tomorrow if the Commission is going to be pleased with my piece on enlightenment. The last time I was saved by my skin colour was getting the honour of being the chief praise-singer at the IMF meeting in Dubai, representing the poets of the South. And my struggle credentials ensured that I am among the few poets and artists whose faces appear on the Official Legends' Hall of Fame built as part of the urban renewal project. But I am not so sure whether I'll do justice to the enlightenment theme. I am not in the habit of planning, scheming, and structuring my poems. Poems come to me while walking in the street, window-shopping, strolling half-naked at the beach, in the middle of the night, on the verge of a climax, in a dream, editing another poem, upon hearing the falling of the first droplet of rain in the first rainfall of the year.

This time around it is a different ball game. I decide to kick-start by finding the literary meaning of enlightenment. All that one can find in the dictionary is "the act of enlightening" So I go to "enlightened" and discover that it means, "to cause to understand", "free from false beliefs". According to me, it is not the belief that has to be true but the believer who has to be true to his belief. For as long as a person's belief in whatever he believes in is true, that is his true belief. Ultimately, there is no false belief, only false believers.

I try hard to jot some lines down on enlightenment, but nothing comes. I am not used to being commissioned to write a poem. I find it a mechanical and rather superficial exercise, sitting down and consciously thinking of the physical beings and mental things associated with the concept, cracking my head to break the concept down into images and sounds.

I remember that my teacher used to unpack a concept by breaking down the word and defining the meaning of each 'sub-word,' finally arriving at his working definition of the meaning of the whole word. So I start looking for "en" and discover that it means "to get into"," to cause to be". "Aha!" I exclaim in relief. And move on to light, which, among other things, means "a natural force that is produced by or redirected from objects and other things, so that we can see them; something that produces such force and causes other things to be seen, the conditions of being or becoming seen or being made known."

Satisfied that I am getting somewhere I quickly search for "ment." No luck until I decide that perhaps "tement" could lead somewhere. In the process of the search my eyes fall on 'temerity', "foolish boldness and rashness". An example: "He had the temerity to demand higher wages after only three days of work." I attempt to put down some ideas on enlightenment, but end with something like: "We have the foolish boldness to search for enlightenment in the library, the temerity to look for the meaning of enlightenment in a dictionary." Perhaps I should go for a cliché and start working on it; sometimes the poet is good at just reworking old clichés and lifting them to the poetic register, aided by poetic license, which sometimes can be nothing less than semantic irresponsibility.

I can only think of one at the moment; "There is light at the end of the tunnel" Ultimately I end up with lines about which I am not sure whether they form a poem or are relevant to the theme. Nevertheless, I switch the computer on and start typing to put the poem into print form.

> *"How do you reach the end?*
> *Or see the light at it*
> *If there is no vision in the tunnel?*
> *The vision does not have to be in the tunnel*
> *It has to be in you*
> *You will carry it with you*
> *And create the light in the tunnel*
> *Sometimes it is not the light that we need*
> *But the tunnel to the light*
> *At times it is not the tunnel*
> *But the vision to the tunnel*
> *Other times it is not the vision*
> *But the man with the vision."*

Shall I take this poem and go to the commission and read it raw as it is, or chop and change and cut and refine until a gem emerges. What makes a piece of writing a gem and who is the final judge? What is the yardstick? Where does a poem start? Does it begin in the mind or in the heart or in the eyes and ears? Sometimes you listen to your heartbeat and feel the rhyme crying out for a vocal tapestry. At times you feel it in your membranes and other times you hear.

the melody ringing in your ears but cannot find the words. Some other times the pictures are fresh in your mind but the lyrics just do not come, or your eyes can visualize the images but your mouth just cannot say it, or you simply cannot think of the metaphors. You might have read about many recipes for writing a poem. But prescribing a recipe for poetry writing is a recipe for a poetic disaster. A poem is not cooked up, nor can it be imported or exported from one person to another. It calls itself into existence at its own time according to its own timing. Sometimes the words flash on your mental screen while you are hooked on the big screen. Other times the rhythm rings in your ears while listening to the rhyme of the sea waves splashing. At times you are tuned to the rhyme by simply listening to the pulse of your heartbeat. Yes, poems have a strange way of rocking up suddenly from nowhere in particular.

I take the podium and face the commission: "I did not manage to write anything on enlightenment but I will think aloud on the subject, maybe a poem will come out of it. Discerning ears are religiously tuned to me as I open my mouth:

"For the fake romance of the self
Human beings have dishonoured
The sacred rite of poetry to turn the holy shrine of storytelling into a gallery
They take the Mic for a lollipop
Licked to draw the attention of the paparazzi
They pose a Colgate smile to dance to the click of the camera
They bask in the spotlight of fame and drown in the echoes of their own voices
They bury their heads in a forest of books
To search for knowledge in the library
And look for enlightenment in a dictionary
They travel from religion to religion in search of the ultimate reality
Emigrate from cult to cult
Questing for a true life
They shall find no enlightenment in a dictionary
They shall meet no Buddha and no Mohammed in a library
Nor shall they see Jesus in a church, mosque or synagogue
They fail to learn the ways of Buddha and Mohammed in the book of real life
They by-pass the wisdom of Jesus in the university of everyday experience
They cannot see the face God in every man and every woman in the street
The rod in the hands of Moses
The spear of Shaka
The harp and the sling of David
The diplomacy of Moshoeshoe
The pen of Fanon and the Mau operations
Are means towards the end
Never to be confused as ends in themselves
Religion is not the way but a way to the way
Culture is not life but a way of life
A stage is not the object but a podium of the arts..."

71.

I receive a standing ovation and an instant invitation to tender to be the premier's official praise-poet, and to send my CV to the committee that is headhunting for a capable man to be the artistic director of the civic theatre. As a mini-test I am requested to rhyme about the local government's Urban Renewal Project and I wax lyrical about it, repressing my inner thoughts that developing the urban areas without similar efforts at the rural level is an exercise in futility.

In the struggle years, when art and culture were weapons of struggle, I quoted a Russian proverb, "When money talks truth becomes silent." The bush echoed my voice and the AKA's applauded. "Let the poet talk," said the chorus. "It is not the poet but God through the poet," explained the believing comrades. The agnostics amended,"God and the poets are one. One is the word in spirit form, the other is spirit in word form." I agreed: "Poetry turns the world round. It was not before Adam and Eve found poetic license to explore for another meaning behind the word wisdom that Labour was born, and labour, Engels said, created Man, and Man, Karl Marx would argue, makes his own history. As to the matter of de-sexing revolutionary language, we shall say humanity makes its own history." The bazooka's applauded and the commander commanded silence. "Let people express their feelings. The people, the poets and the combatants are one," argued the commissars, quoting Brecht. I smiled.

For the record, I have never carried a gun. I was recruited strictly for the movement's cultural wing, to boost the morale of the army, to coin revolutionary slogans and compose relevant songs, to be the cultural ambassador of the movement and raise some funds. My rise and rise as the wordsmith of the movement earned me the title of Revolutionary Poet, now called the African Renaissance Poet. I spent more time on tours and was only summoned to the bush in moments of tragedy when I had to console the comrades who had lost their fellow cadres in an ambush, a booby trap or a mysterious disappearance.

Otherwise I travelled the world. I graced Zimbabwe freedom celebration, the Oscar awards, Prince Charles' marriage, Madiba's 70th birthday anniversary and many more such events. I ended up falling for Boy George (or did he fall for me?) Oh boy, did I screw him... I must stop this nonsense reminiscence. Just now my wife returns from the bathroom, she is a well-respected business lady, you know. I first met her at the Comrade Mayor's wedding. Just think of it, there were times when poetry could land you in shit. These days you can find yourself with your bums in honey.

Look at my case, there was I, reading a few lines from my new collection of love poems, when out of the blue I got a request from the managing director of an affluent firm to do radio and TV commercials for their products. (Way back in the struggle years, I railed against blaxploitation and the commercialisation of the arts. I predicted a cultural renaissance in Africa and the South: "Like we foiled the grenades in the bush, we shall spoil the ploys of the coin in the arts.") My TV advert was a hit. I had relied on politically correct language, my mellow voice, and a bit of humour and wit plus acting experience. Overnight I was a god in my country and no longer a totally forgotten returnee from exile and an unknown prophet. Suddenly my face was all over the screen. Children began to sing my name. They walked, talked, dressed, laughed and even made love like I do. "I Drink Coke to smile like the Renaissance man" Use this condom; this is what the Renaissance Poet uses."

Book 2

BOFELOSOPHY

Essays and Reviews

HYBRIDAZATION AND SLANG IN SOUTH AFRICAN POETRY: A CURSORY LOOK AT IKE MUILA'S "GOVA" AND FAROUK ASVAT'S "BRA FROOKS"

Abstract

Focusing on Ike Muila's **"Gova"** and Farouk Asvat's **"Bra Frooks"**, this essay locates the use of hybridization and slang in South African Poetry within the context of the contestation of space between dominant/established and subaltern/ marginalized/ previously underground discourses, and relates it to the search for forms of literary expression attuned to the realities of post-apartheid, neo-colonial South Africa and the 'globalized world.' It takes into cognizance the discourses on the politics of language in literature and the relationship between the dominance of the English Language and the English colonial project.

English and the colonial and de-colonization project

The dominant position of English in Southern Africa (as is the case in many parts of the world) is both the product and instrument of the English colonial project. Introduced into South Africa in the 19th century by colonial soldiers, administrators, missionaries, settlers and fortune-seekers, English established itself as Southern African as a result of the settlements of 1820 (Eastern Cape), and 1848-1862 (Natal), and the discovery of the diamond mines of Kimberley (1870) and the gold mines of Witwatersrand (1886). It entered the Black Community through missionary activities, particularly with its use as a medium of instruction in mission schools. English then managed to entrench itself as the dominant language in politics, literature, business and academia in South Africa from the time it was pronounced as the sole official language of the Cape Colony in 1882, with concerted efforts to establish it as the sole language of law and education even in predominately Dutch/Afrikaans speaking districts. This dominant position of English was consolidated by the mission school's creation of an articulate Black English speaking elite that included writers, academics, leaders and politicians as well as the adoption of English as the official medium of instruction by the liberation movement. (See Safron, Hall. **South African English in post-Apartheid era: Hybridization in Zoë Wicomb's David's Story and Ivan Vladislavic's the Restless Supermarket)**

Through the influence of Negritude, Africanism, Afro-centricism and Black Consciousness, the notion of challenging dominant English linguistic and literary conventions came to be perceived as an integral part of the de-colonization project. The paths pursued by writers who sought to subvert the dominance of Standard English and English literary conventions included writing in African languages, breathing African idiomatic, aesthetic, literary and artistic expressions into English, and the use of hybridization - the mix of languages (and genres) - and township slang.

Language in literature

Former South African president, Nelson Mandela, once asserted that if one speaks to a person in a language s/he understands, one appeals to that person's mind, but if one speaks in that person's language one appeals to that person's heart. This statement resonates with the discourse arguing that to reach the masses it is imperative that Africa promote the use of indigenous languages in literature, academia and politics. But since literature is an articulation of the individual and collective memory and imagination of a people and an expression of both a personal and social voice, reaching out to people in literature may require being more in tandem with their lived reality and socio-conceptual framework, rather than merely talking to them in their mother tongue. The Mthembus of Alexandra and the Mthembus of Sandton, as well as the Masekos in the village of Lesotho and the Masekos in Deepkloof in Soweto, may share a mother tongue but they do not share the language of real life experience. Though they may speak in one language the rich and the poor do not talk the same language. The Sesotho/ Isizulu/Xintsonga, English/ Afrikaans and slang (and feminism) of a domestic worker from rural South Africa has its own nuances and colors that are very distinct from that of the female CEO from Houghton. The slang of Township South Africa has myriad templates and tones because Chartsworth and Sebokeng and Soweto and Gugulethu and Kwamashu are not the same.

Literature in any society has a variety of accents and templates because the reality of being female and young in the world is not the same as the reality of being male and adult in the world; just as the experience of being disabled and poor is not the same as that of being disabled and rich. Likewise the reality of being Black in the world is not the same as the reality of being White in the world, the reality of being Black, poor and working class is different from the experience of being Black, middle-class or bourgeois in post-Apartheid neo-colonial, liberal capitalist South Africa.

But things are not either Black or White. I found out more about and the reality of being Black, marginalized, disempowered and downtrodden in the world from the poetry of Wokpo Jensma than I could in the works of Black writers whose works in African languages-were prescribed for us in schools. I remember reading a glowing poetic tribute to Verwoed in Sesotho. Something to this effect *"O titime o thswanelwa ke moqhaka wa thlolo"* (You have run, you deserve the crown of victory) Though Wokpo Jensma was White and was writing in English, and writers like this one who showered Verwoed with praises had Black skins and were writing in my mother tongue, it is the former rather than the latter who reached my heart. And my mind found it nonsensical that a Black man could waste ink and time, not only in mourning the death of the architect of Apartheid but also declaring him a hero.

Even if Mandela were to use IsiXhosa to refer to the wife of Verwoed as the wife of a hero or Mbeki was to confer heroic status on Matanzima, Treunicht and their ilk in Sesotho, this would still not appeal to the minds and hearts of people who speak these languages. Biko, Fanon and Cabral spoke to me in English and appealed to both my heart and mind. Fela Kuti sang in Pidgin English and moved the masses of people across cultures around the globe. Sipho Sepamla's Xhosa-English, the Zunglish of Phila Myeni and Ike Muila's Iscamtho poetry filled with Tshivenda idioms talk to the man and woman in the streets of Azania. (South Africa).

The language of real life experience and the language of literature

To put it simply, for literature to move people it must not only make linguistic and grammatical sense but should also speak to their conditions and experiences. It is not accidental that while arguing for literature in indigenous African languages, Ngungi wa Thiongo is also a protagonist of literature that is deeply embedded in the concrete and tangible historical-material realities of a people. This type of literature is grounded in social reality and is therefore part and parcel of the individual and collective struggle of people to be and to belong. For Ngungi wa Thiongo it is imperative that the literature that captures this language of real life experience be expressed in the language of the people so that it can also contribute to enriching and enhancing these languages, thereby boosting the collective dignity and self-esteem of communities and cultures to which these languages belong.

On the other hand Harry Mashabela and others have argued that if people like Biko, Fanon and Cabral had written in their ethnic languages, their writings, thoughts, philosophies and theories would not have been accessible to the multitudes of people they were able to reach by writing in English, French and Portuguese. Ngungi wa Thiongo addresses this concern by using the medium of translations to reach out to the universal family of humankind. He argues that weaving African proverbial, idiomatic, aesthetic and literary expressions into English results in the enrichment and development of English rather than the enrichment and development of the African languages. While others have argued that a lot is lost in translation, it is important to note that translation is in itself the dialogue of languages and cultures. Therefore writing literature in one language and translating it into another results in the enrichment of both languages, instead of a one-way process whereby one language feeds on the other. In practical terms this amounts to the conversation of peoples and cultures. Thus Ngungi wa Thiong'o championing of the translation from one African language to another in addition to translating from African languages to European languages is something that African governments, academic institutions, literary practitioners and publishers should encourage.

But as I have argued from the beginning, the people's language is more than language in the strict linguistic sense. It includes the people's everyday socio-cultural, politico-economic reality and cultural experiences- the fears and hopes, dreams and nightmares, aspirations and frustrations, illusions and disillusions, as well as the fantasies and imaginations of people as individuals and as a collective. This is because language, as a means and medium of a human being's interaction and engagement with fellow humanity and the world around him/her, is a social construct and is therefore a signifier and mirror of socio-politico-economic and historical-material realities and socio-cultural, personal and community experiences. Therefore the individual and collective memory and imagination of a people as expressed through their language, culture, literature and arts is grounded in these experiences and realities. Since history and social and personal experience is not static, linguistic, literary, aesthetic and idiomatic expressions are subject to a dynamic process of inventiveness, innovativeness, and ingenuity to articulate the nuances, particularities and peculiarities of a specific historical, geo-political, socio-cultural, politico-economic context and individual and/or collective experience.

Hybridization and slang language

This brings us to the fact that in a multi-cultural, cosmopolitan society like South Africa the language of real life experience includes the meeting and conversation of languages and cultures and therefore the development of slang as a lingua franca of the man and woman in the street. The street language; Iscamtho, Ringas, Flytaal; 'Tsotsitaal, incorporates Africanized articulations of English and Afrikaans; 'Pidgin English' and 'Kombuis Afrikaans.' and Indo-Pakistani accentuated English. The underworld, the campus community, the taxi industry, fishermen, pilots, the worker and the elite, as well as the poet and the musician…. each of these has their own accent and adds something to South African slang.

Inevitably this language has become part and parcel of popular culture. It influences and is influenced by popular culture and all the sub-cultures that can be found in society. It therefore was only natural that this mixing of cultures –an expression of the cultural melting pot that South Africa has become- would take place in South African literature and popular music.

In the 70's, Black Consciousness writers like Mothubi Motloatse and Sipho Sipamla went beyond the grammatical and literary conventions of English in search of a poetry that spoke in the voice of a child from the streets of Khayelitsha, Soweto and Gugulethu. While Motloatse and others experimented with a fusion of prose, poetry, music and drama, Sipamla mixed English and Isixhosa. Farouk Asvat and Adam Small experimented with Kombuis Afrikaans and Indo-Pak English, with Small also reclaiming pure Afrikaans as the language of the common man, breathing the cry of freedom into this language that had been hijacked by Herrenvolkism. As far back as the period between the 50's and the early 70's, popular South African musical genres like jazz, marabi and mbaqanga had lyrics in African languages. Disco and Afro-pop of the late 70's and 80's mixed African languages, English and a bit of street language.

The Kwaito era

The 90's saw the emergence of the dance music genre called Kwaito, which while tapping into rap beats, house rhythms and opening itself up to the influences of jazz and at times using rhythm and blues harmonies, also draw from the aesthetic rhythms of earlier musical genres, characterized by the resonance of the drum and bass that gives it a distinct African flavour.

To give its voice a more South African accent kwaito drew extensively on the vast well of vernaculars of South Africa and the many variants of township slang. According to Aryan Kaganof the hybrid nature of kwaito reflects its proclivity to resolve the dialectic between struggle culture and bubblegum, pure entertainment and art for a socio-political purpose, by fusing these previously opposed tendencies in township politics, positing sophisticated, digital body liberation whereby dancing itself becomes the site for a radical rejection of the traditional struggle lyrics in favour of the liberation of pleasure, while at the same time attempting to use the language of the street to grapple with and articulate the present reality for the man and woman in the streets of the ghetto and to explore the future. (See: Sharp-Sharp: The Kwaito Story)
(http://kaganof.com/kagablog/category/films/sharp-sharp-the-kwaito-story/)

Kwaito star, Zola (Bonginkosi Dlamini) posits that the kwaito concept of mixing languages to produce a sort of lingua franca that facilitates interaction and communication between people from different socio-linguistic and cultural backgrounds dates as far back as the days of the establishment of the Cape Colony. *"It all begins with the Dutch people. The voyagers when they come to South Africa and then all the other nations mix up as South Africans integrate into what it becomes today but basically you had Dutch which of course when it mixed up with other languages ended up as a language called Afrikaans and in Afrikaans there's a word called kwaai, sommer baie gevaarlik, somebody who's dangerous, like very cheeky you know, hard core. And then back in the sixties there was a gangster groups called Amakwaitos which of course were the most notorious boys around. I don't know exactly if they were from Sophiatown or Soweto, one of the two, but that's basically where the name came from. So we had a bit of Afrikaans a bit of Zulu a bit of English a bit of Tswana Tsonga Tshona and then all those languages came up together when people started working in the mines when people went up to Jo'burg with the gold rush and then they had their own language. That's where the name kwai came from and as the years went by music changed and it ended up being called kwaito as in Amakwaitos."* (Zola in an interview with Aryan Kaganof)

Language in post-1994 poetry

In the literary arena, the search for forms of artistic and aesthetic expression that capture the peculiarities and particularities of the social issues, challenges and opportunities of post – Apartheid South Africa, coming with its own set of promises and contradictions, dreams and nightmares, fears and hopes, peculiarities and particularities of the contradictions, saw the growth of poetry among young people. This also came with an exploration of new stylistic and thematic concerns, which ranged from experimenting with hip hop, dub/reggae and jazz poetic accents, to tapping into African orature, and delving into the fluidity, spontaneity, vibrancy and vastness/richness of the ghetto-lingo; Iscamtho/Ringas, Flytaal.

Sometimes poets write mainly in English and bring in either jazz/blues/soul aspects, or Rasta-speak, ragga rhythms or dub beats, or slam poetry and hip hop beats, or ghetto lingo and kwaito sounds, or traditional African oral, or all of these influences. Though some poets choose to specialize in one of the genres and are quite comfortable with being classified as 'page' poet or 'performance poet', spoken word artist, 'slam poet' oral poet, 'praise -poet', etc   many poets, including those who are referred to in the media by some of these labels, choose not to confine themselves to any template or label. Therefore you find a significant number of poets who write for both the page and the stage and who also have collections of poems that are a mixture of poems written in English, and poems written in hybrid language, Rasta-speak, the hip hop register, African languages, Iscamtho/Tsotsitaal and a mix of these.

Ike Muila's Iscamtho poetry:

Though there is an increase in the number of poets with poems that utilize hybridization, fusing English and African languages with slang/Iscamtho, Rasta and rapspeak, Ike Mboneni Muila of the Botsotso Jesters is probably the only South African poet who writes/performs solely in a mix of languages, and is very passionate, irrepressible and unrepentant in calling the playful mixing of languages and slanguages, the samplings of folk-songs and children's tales and snap-shots of township and village scenes, art/poetry: *"I am into creative writing as a poet artist performer/ my narrative mix is in eleven languages spoken in South Africa/ by and bye trapped in one poem / the so called tsetse tail/ iscamtho lingo alive and kicking sense of humor in you and me/ mixing of languages into a witty lingo/ a language of identity/ a language of an ordinary person in the street/ a language of unity in diversity."*

His poems boldly declare that his mission is to make art/poetry out of the mixing of languages and slanguages, out of the recollection, reconstruction, re-mixing and adaptation of children's game-songs, folk songs/African classics games/songs/township classics/township tales and the exposition of everyday real-life stories in the streets, villages, townships and inner cities of Azania. As if in response to critics who question the literary-ness/originality, like fellow poet Lesego Rampolokeng who charged him with *writing his arse in Sophiatown, back spinning in dj mode, cutting and pasting to copyright children's game-songs by taking them off the ground and locking them in a book,* Ike Muila pronounces in a tongue-in-cheek poem, aptly titled 'Velevele':

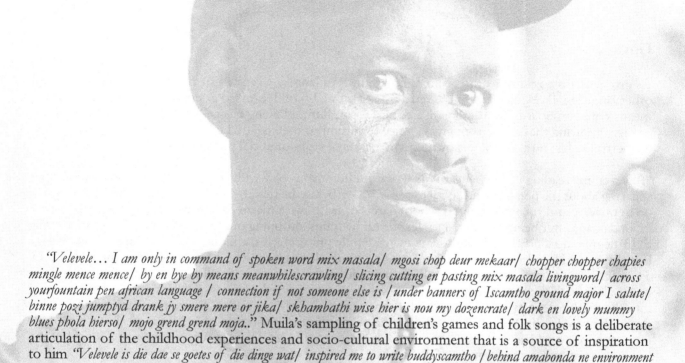

"*Velevele… I am only in command of spoken word mix masala/ mgosi chop deur mekaar/ chopper chopper chapies mingle mence mence/ by en bye by means meanwhilescrawling/ slicing cutting en pasting mix masala livingword/ across yourfountain pen african language / connection if not someone else is /under banners of Iscamtho ground major I salute/ binne pozi jumptyd drank jy smere mere or jika/ skhambathi wise hier is nou my dozencrate/ dark en lovely mummy blues phola hierso/ mojo grend grend moja..*" Muila's sampling of children's games and folk songs is a deliberate articulation of the childhood experiences and socio-cultural environment that is a source of inspiration to him "*Velevele is die dae se goetes of die dinge wat/ inspired me to write buddyscamtho /behind amabonda ne environment ya se kasi langikhulela khona as a bambino had an/ all-round inspiring impact on me a lot/ playing hide and seek black mampatile no no game*"

The characters in his poems are not caricatures, mere figments of the poet's imagination, but real people walking the streets of Mofolo and Venda. These people are not the robots and stereotypes we meet on TV and in the newspapers, but people with diverse personalities, dreams and hopes, and they have a history, of which the story of Sophiatown, Skom and Fietas and the forced removals is an integral part:"*..people I associate with are amongst gawe mense/ comrade bras tigers van ou topies en taimas/ wat slim is/ a bo matwetwe mogoe se clever one site/ kom kry hulle dra die dae se vision forward ennet/ soos hulle is capable to lead the way soos mense/ wat ken hulle mission in life as buddys/ van toeka se dae vele.*"

For Ike, Iscamtho is not about a show of loquaciousness and playing with words. It is an expression of a people's way of living:"*velevele…nomakanjani mr know it al/ ndangala spy poet in supreme isicamtho is a language of survival no wordplay about vele Velevele…*"

Gova

As proof of his commitment to claiming Iscamtho as a language capable of producing literature like any other language, Ike Muila has published a book (with CD) of Iscamtho poetry entitled **'Gova'**, which means come on board. Responding in a critical essay, Rampolokeng has called **'Gova'** a chorus without a voice, implying that apart from giving voice to Iscamtho the lingo, which is public and not private property, Ike has no voice of his own, or any personal story or social message to present.

However, my reading is that beneath the witty and humorous play with language, there is a personal voice speaking about the personal and social experiences of being the heir to victims of forced removal, growing up in poverty and squalor, going to school barefoot, with iwisa maize meal for trousers, suffering severe brain damage after being clobbered to near death by thugs, dropping out from university while attempting a BA degree in Education, with reflections on family photographs, childhood friendships, Venda village landscapes and mindscapes, and conversations with the loved ones who have gone on to the next world. Then there are township scenes: people puffing and pushing bottle-kops all day long, moving around the house along with the sun, cigarettes and dagga skyf passing from the owner to the parasite, others escaping into the world of partying, gluttony and consumerism- braai vleis and beer, people drinking and eating themselves to death. Yes, the Iscamtho language and Kofifi register that Ike Muila speaks in, is not his property —you could as well hear/imagine Don Mattera and Can Themba when tuning to 'Gova'-but the unique accent, pulse, vibe, energy of Ike is there.

Ike may not be an overtly political poet but the power of his pronouncements on socio-economic and political issues lies in its subtlety, wit and in the ordinariness of the language, the everydayness of its scenery and the familiarity of the images, sounds and rhythms and the fluidity of its stylistic accomplishment. The poem "I stare in wonder" best captures Muila's ability to bring together myriad worlds and a confluence of worldviews and possibilities through a mix of language and a deliberate eschewing of structure. A surreal depiction of the kitschy frivolity of mass culture, the social decay, brutalization, naked criminality and identity crisis in urban/township SA is juxtaposed with a graphic portrayal of Venda village landscapes and mindscapes.

"I stare in wonder
Stockings kilometer burn jive grand
Party house management pulling out
Stinking boots en knicker bandage of the country
Socks entitled by naked future feminique
Striking no strings attached
The love fencing spear head tumbler
Within a bottomless maxosha shacks
Unknown rough and ugly
Ginger four manyawo pause a threat
To innocent heart broken container
I stare in wonder
Jack roller without a heart driven gwavhavha
Bo daai dairy fortress children of asazi kopa
I stare in wonder
Kom kry haak vry staat get mchovana
Spoon down test
The silver cup is broken
If you see a stop sign lapha site
Shova take no u-turn
Qalaza syndicate then
Short left or short right
Waya waya niks mabuya joe
My bracade verstaan my mnca
Van die one-one
Jy slaat my dizzy wrong site
Moen skokkend werk mabone jive
Deedum dum
Dummy table
I stare in wonder
Them sluggish fat cow smoking a zol
Bo dae joint outside the backyard wood
Resembling them erring bulls without horns
Sharing a blade in the ghetto jol
I stare in wonder
A drievoet face dose of marijuana
Monkey do smoking a home made pipe
Like a bottle kop shova
I stare in wonder

Looking at mutavhatsindi camp
Nearby Makonde mountain range
When it dawned in my mind
That a mother insectivorous plant does exist
Which preys on anything alive even in human beings
Who dare go nearby the tree
No wonder it is believed
You could only escape mutavhatsindi catch
If and only if you go nearby naked to the tree
I stare in wonder
Failing to escape the loudness in my mind
My in in-law Mulamu and I turned to listen
With all that funny feelings jogging in my mind
To Bob Marley's reggae music in a car
Music with the philosophy of generations yet to come by
And ponder about war in the Middle East, of nation war against nation
I stare in wonder still
Cruising all over the mutale region
Surrounded by the Makonde mountain range
Melandi and takalani in the back seat of a car
Singing a Venda version of one of Bob Marley's songs
Indeed…
Vha na gonova vha thsikhalani"

Bra Frooks

The only other poet to have published a poetry book of slang language is Farouk Asvat, a medical doctor and one of the prominent Black Consciousness writers in the 70's. The difference between the two is that while Muila's book is the product of a decade of writing solely in Iscamtho, Asvat's book - entitled **'Bra Frooks'** - is a collection of poems gleaned from his previous books, which contained predominantly English poems, and a few new poems that were not featured in previous collections. In addition to publishing Bra Frooks, Farouk Asvat has included English translations of his slang poems in his revised copies of his book, **"Time of our Lives."**

In **Bra Frooks**, Asvat uses witty, humorous, sarcastic and satiric language to expose the contradictions, emotional terrains and tensions in both Apartheid and post-Apartheid South Africa. He uses the lingo, voice and logic of the man and woman in the street to expose the absurdity of political repression and social control and the mediocrity and hypocrisy of political and religious dogmatism. The tenacity and resilience of people in the face of repression and suppression is exhibited by their ability to see the humorous side of every situation, laughing at the short-sightedness of their oppressors as well as having a good laugh at themselves. This playfulness and wittiness of slang language comes in handy, especially where Asvat uses narrative, monologue, dialogue/dramatic techniques, as in "Bra Frooks en die John Voster Span', 'Ou China en die Amper-Intellectual', 'Las' Bus', 'Ek het nie Gepolitiek, my Baas', 'Die Volk Broer', 'Boza', and 'Over the Wall an' All'.

The concerns and interests of the poorest people on the ground are contrasted with the theorizing and philosophizing of the kamma intellectuals, the opulent new captains of capital and their friends in government, and the petit and aspirant bourgeoisie:

"Boza! Jy het die kar
En jy het die sjheld, boza!
En ek, ek het die fok'all
S'trues god! Boza,
Ons is nie die Mandela's
Ons soek net n' paar cents
Om die brood the koop my Koning
Wan'my mag hy huil
Ag please, Boza
Ek wil nes die Mandelas:
N' bloed rooi Mercedes
N' spier wit mansion
En Amandla!
Georgio Armani!
Awethu!"

Asvat manages to use slang satirically and humorously to provide insight into matters as complex as the dynamics and contradictions of identity (be it ethnic, socio-economic, linguistic or religious), and into issues as delicate and sensitive as race and human frailty, ritualistic religiosity and religious hypocrisy.

"Allah-hu-taala het gesê innie Koran
Djulle moet djulle bekke hou
Preek die Imam innie smokkelhuis;
Hoek me Allah
Djkr hy by die jintoe
Wat net halaal kos iet
Toe excommunicate die jamma hom.
Maa' Allah ken mos betere
Wan' die man het hom mos geremember
Ennie woord gespread tussen innie mense
En toe stuur Allah hom straight heaven toe
Met n' borrel dop."

For the uninitiated here is the English translation:

"Allah the highest said in the Qur'an
You must keep your moth shut
The Imam preaches in the shebeen
Hook-me-Allah
He chants at the harlot
Who only eats halaal food.

So the community excommunicated him
But Allah knows much better
Because the man remembered him
And spread the word in-between the people.
And so Allah sent him, straight to heaven
With a bottle of booze."

Conclusion

"Gova" and **"Bra Frooks"** are examples of using the language of the street to reclaim the right of ordinary people to articulate their personal and collective experiences under their conditions and in their terms, in the language attuned to their everyday reality and through the lingo that is a product of their experiential and existential reality and is therefore shaped and informed by their environment. The use of slang/hybrid language is in itself a subversive act, both from a literary and political point of view... Going beyond established English grammar and literary conventions amounts to challenging the dominant discourses on language and literature as well as contesting Eurocentric perspectives of language and literature.

Hybridization is one of the ways by which previously marginalized voices are contesting the dominance of Standard English. Hall Saffron observes that through hybridization the English language undergoes the simultaneous process of devolution and renewal, disempowerment and reinvigoration akin to the revitalization of Latin as a result of travestying in the era of the Renaissance. This, Saffron asserts, amounts to putting English in today's South Africa into a state of becoming rather than of being. While South Africans accent the English language with their own idiomatic, aesthetic and literary expression of social reality, thereby enriching it in the process, some words (and therefore concepts) from indigenous African languages and some slang ultimately get integrated into the English lexicon. But for the artist who express him/herself in hybrid/slang lingo the most important issue is claiming the right to name/ label and define things, the right to define the world around him/her according to his/her terms. The poet who writes in Iscamtho/ township slang finds the same sense of self-fulfillment and self-reaffirmation from making the 'ghetto lingo' the language of literature, science and academia in the same way that the protagonist of Afro-centricity would find self-affirmation, dignity and integrity by producing a work of literature, an academic dissertation or scientific research paper in an African language.

REFERENCES

1   Asvat, Farouk. 2006. **Bra Frooks.** Piquant Publishing: Fordsburg
2.   Botsotso 13
3.   Botsotso 14
4   Kaganof, Aryan. Sharp-Sharp: The Kwaito Story (http://kaganof.com/kagablog/category/films/sharp-sharp-the-kwaito-story/) accessed on 20\11\2007
5.   Muila, Ike.2006.**Gova.**Botsotso Publishing: Johannesburg
6.   Safron, Hall. South African English in post-Apartheid era: Hybridization in Zoë Wican's David's Story and Ivan Vladislavic's The Restless Supermarket (www.africanstudies.uct.ac.zapostamble/vol2-1/english.pdf) accessed on 20\11\2007

BRENDA AND GENDER

Disco was the music and the lines of divide between the pantsula and the hippie and the cats and the ivies were crystal clear. You did not talk the talk if you could not walk the walk and be spot-on as far as the dress was concerned. The dress and the walk and the talk said it all. There were no neutrals, no idle critics and no passive spectator on the floor. As long as you could talk, you could sing and as long as you could walk, you could dance. A serenading, mellow-melodious voice and a rhythmic beat expressed a woman's frustration with a love relationship in which she played second fiddle- a weekend special.
"You don't come around to see me in the week
You do not find the time to call me on the phone
But Friday night I know I must be ready for you… "

The jietas and cherries responded accordingly, singing along and falling into crazy, aerobic, acrobatic choreographic moves. A majivani put a beer-bottle on his foot and kicked it up into his hands and onto his lips, shaking the head, swaying his behind and getting down till he was the size of a king-size coke-cola bottle. A mshoza got down to do it for the ladies. Her phenduka skirt gave her the freedom to be a butterfly and the old timers gleefully cheered her on "Saak, my kind! Phenduka, Mtwana!" "Dlala ngekepana! Lahla'umleze uzothola'umendo." A manocha jitterbugged with a chair on his head, another guluva grooved on a chair, others on the table and some twisted and bumped against each other. On the floor it was the battle of the Saxons, Commandos and the Buccaneers, the Moccasins and Crocket & Jones and the Perry Cardins and Carduccis. Ululations and whistles in the air.

The weekend newspaper carried a story about the young woman singer who had blasted out her pop-disco sounds and exhibited her suggestive dances inside Regina Mundi Church. The movement defended her as the show was a fund-raiser for the struggle, but some critics castigated the music as bubble-gum-loud, sweet-for-nothing empty lyrics. The outhies and bo-mshoza were more interested in which tune took out the best in them on the dance floor. Some went crazy as they sang sing "Last night a deejay saved my life", and others got into trance singing: "It's nice to be with people". This was the eighties. And Yvonne Chakachaka and Brenda Fassie & the Big Dudes (and Mercy Phakela, Cheek to Cheek, and Splash) were the hottest items in town – and Sello "Chicco" Thwala, Kamazu, Paul Ndlovu, Peter Tenet and Dan Tshanda were die ouens van die stuk. It was the era of style, elegance and wits, survival skills and basic instinct. It was either you had a zi-4 and were a majiyane to lie your way out, or you had inkane to bully your way out ngedlondlo and ngedlovu yangena. Only the clever and the strong and brave and bold dared to be who and what they wanted to be.

No one characterized the era with a distinct chutzpa and hell of pluck, mkgaga and mokgopolo as Brenda Fassie. From the dusty streets of Langa she made her way out onto the hurly-burly and hustle-bustle of Jozi life and in the ntja eja ntjanyana world of Show Busnix- a business in which you give your all but are left with fokkol & nix. But more, Ma-Brr will be remembered for unsettling societal notions of femininity and womanhood. In a society were woman are simply the beautiful, sexy pictures that make good magazine posters and exquisite adverts, Brenda took the right of the individual over her body beyond the limits and de-limits of sex /gender, and became a pioneer of sex-blindness in South Africa / Azania. She certainly was not the proverbial barefooted and pregnant girl, the typical dutiful and happily married woman or the advertorial Colgate-smile beauty following the scent of exotic deodorant under the Casanova's armpit.

Where most women cover themselves in a Mill & Boons novel and wait for the proverbial prince charming to swipe them off their feet, Brenda picked and dumped, (some will say hired, fired and re-hired) lovers-male and female- when and as she wanted. She expressed her love (and her lust) anytime, anywhere and every-how- the way only she could have done it. Where many will speak in hushed tones about their sex lives and their performance in bed, Brenda was extravagantly open and ostentatious about her libido. Whenever she parted ways with one of her male and female lovers, Ma-Brr… was often quick to claim the partner was too lousy in bed and could not match her performance standards.

She often told journalists "I am hot". Very often she also told the scribes where to get off and when to shut their loud mouths and close their inquisitive eyes…. Slapping a few unlucky one's in the process. Unrestrained, unpredictable and rapid in her actions, straightforward in the way she talked but very fluid and flexible as far as her love and sex life is concerned. Very exhibitionist as far as her body and her sexuality was concerned. She was also very spontaneous and dramatic… Like when at a show in the belly of the beast- the USA (the Unite States of Anything goes) she bared her breasts and excitedly told the audience: "This is Africa!" That was Ma Brr. The Black Madonna- an unconfined, uncontainable, irrepressible symbol of non-conformity and non-homophobia. Audacious. Outspoken. Carefree…Reckless!

Gramsci and Biko on Hegemony and Counter-hegemony and the Role of Intellectuals and Mass Participation

"The starting point of critical elaboration is the consciousness of what one really is …the mode of being of the new intellectual can no longer consist in eloquence but in active participation in practical life, as constructor, organizer, "permanent persuader" and not just a simple orator…"

-Antonio Gramsci

"The most potent weapon in the hands of the oppressors is the mind of the oppressed"

-Stephen Bantu Biko / Frantz Fanon

Introduction

Antonio Gramsci' s expositions on the notion of hegemony; the use of both coercion and consent to sustain power and maintain the status quo and on the role of traditional and organic intellectuals and the significance of mass participation in building a counter hegemony offers us a great understanding of the role of civil society together with religious, labour, cultural, social and political movements and informal educators in transforming traditional forms of education and challenging the right of the dominant class to rule.

This essay discusses Gramsci' s ideas on ideology / hegemony and counter-hegemony, organic intellectuals and mass participation and examines the extent to which Stephen Bantu Biko and the Black Consciousness Movement took into cognizance the role of ideology and the consent of the oppressed Black people in maintaining the status quo in Apartheid South Africa, and presented psychological liberation and mental emancipation, self-realization, self-reliance and Black Solidarity as essential elements of a counter-hegemony to white supremacism and a sine quo non for the replacement of Apartheid-Capitalism with an egalitarian and anti-racist society.   Our point of departure is the idea that civil society organizations; religious institutions, cultural, social and political movements, labour organizations, non-governmental organizations and social clubs, etc have the potential to be turned into organs of working class power- facilitating bottom-up, grassroots-oriented and participatory democracy by providing the underclass with spaces, platforms and avenues, not to mention strategies, skills, expertise, methods and mechanisms through which they can challenge the establishment, place demands on power and contest its hegemony.

These groups can also be an effective means of imparting alternative information, knowledge and education that challenges the information, knowledge and education transmitted by mainstream educational institutions and the corporate media to entrench the philosophy, culture, ethics, mores and values of the dominant ruling class so as to conserve the status quo. The converse is also true; civil society organizations; religious, cultural, labour, social and political movements can also serve to legitimatize the powers that be and preserve the status quo by restricting people to a reformist agenda geared only to searching for solutions within the confines of the prevailing system, instead of exploring possibilities of transforming, reconstructing and overhauling the system.

To put it in simple terms, by virtue of their involvement in advocacy, lobbying, awareness-raising, training programmes and interventions in issues related to policy formulation, civil society organizations like non-governmental organizations (NGOs), community-based organizations (CBOs), social movements, religious institutions, cultural clubs and societies are an integral part of social institutions and agencies contributing to the process of education and socialization- i.e. the re-establishment and re-enforcement of the prevailing and dominant norms-and-value system in a society. This means, in effect, that the role of these organizations and institutions is either to legitimise the prevailing socio-economic and political system and maintain the status quo or to question the current dispensation and offer alternative ways of conceptualizing social reality and organizing society for the collective good of all of humanity and the preservation of the entire earth.

Ideological Hegemony

While Gramsci accepted the analysis of capitalism put forward by Marx in the previous century and accepted that the struggle between the ruling class and the subordinate working class was the driving force that moved society forward, he did not embrace the traditional very one-sided Marxist theory of power based on the role of force and coercion as the basis of ruling class domination. He pointed out the role played by ideology in legitimizing the differential power that groups hold and concentrated on the power of the subtle but pervasive forms of ideological control and manipulation that served to perpetuate all repressive structures. He identified two quite distinct forms of political control: domination, which referred to direct physical coercion by the police and armed forces, and hegemony, which referred to both ideological control and more crucially, consent through the permeation throughout society of an entire system of values, attitudes, beliefs and morality that has the effect of maintaining the status quo in power relations. (Burke, B. (1999) 'Antonio Gramsci and informal education', the encyclopedia of informal education, http://www.infed.org\thinkers\et-gram.htm)

Positing hegemony as the 'organizing principle' that is diffused by the process of socialization into every area of daily life, Gramsci assumed that no regime, regardless of how authoritarian it might be, could sustain itself primarily through organized state power and armed force, as it ultimately needs popular support and legitimacy in order to maintain stability. He asserts that this prevailing consciousness is internalized by the population to the extent that it becomes part of what is generally called 'common sense' so that the philosophy, culture and morality of the ruling elite comes to appear as the natural order of things. (Boggs 1976: 39)

Gramsci took Marx's basic division of society into a base represented by the economic structure and a superstructure represented by the institutions and beliefs prevalent in society further by dividing the superstructure into those institutions that were overtly coercive and those that were not. He identified the coercive ones as the public institutions such as the government, police, armed forces and the legal system, which he referred to as the state or political society and the non-coercive ones as the churches, the schools, trade unions, political parties, cultural associations, clubs, the family etc. which he regarded as civil society. To a certain extent, schools could fit into both categories, as parts of school life are quite clearly coercive(compulsory education, the national curriculum, national standards and qualifications) whilst others are not (the hidden curriculum).

Gramsci extrapolated from the Marxist notion of society as composed of the base (the mode of economy and the relationship between labour and capital) and the superstructure (external manifestations of the system and the instrument of class control –the government, the army, the police and social institutions like schools, churches, etc), to articulate a subtle theory of power that explained how the ruling class ruled courtesy of productive relations(capital versus labour); coercive institutions (the state or political society) and civil society and all other non-coercive institutions. This provided an understanding of why the European working class had on the whole failed to develop revolutionary consciousness after the First World War and had instead moved towards reformism; i.e. tinkering with the system rather than working towards overthrowing it.

Having asserted that the ruling class maintained its domination by the consent of the mass of the people and only used its coercive apparatuses- the forces of law and order- in the last resort, and that the hegemony of the ruling capitalist class resulted from an ideological bond between the rulers and the ruled, Gramsci addressed the question of the possibility of overthrowing the system or breaking the ideological bond by arguing that revolutionaries have to build up a 'counterhegemony' to that of the ruling class.

To this end, Gramsci argued that structural change and ideological change should be seen as part of the same struggle. He maintained that while the labour process was at the core of the class struggle, it was the ideological struggle that had to be addressed if the mass of the people were to come to a level of consciousness that allowed them to question their political and economic masters' right to rule. In other words, popular consensus in civil society has to be challenged. Thus he emphasized the role of informal education in overcoming the popular consensus that accrues from the fact that the ideological hegemony in place causes the majority of the population to accept what is happening in society as 'common sense' or as 'the only way of running society'. The role of the counterhegemony is to instil the capacity to think critically with a view to altering the whole system based on unequal power-relations between labour and capital and the commodification of labour and the means of production, instead of only complaining about the way things are run and calling for improvements or reforms while embracing the basic beliefs and value system underpinning society as either neutral or of general applicability in relation to the class structure of society. In other words, the purpose of the counter-hegemony is to heighten and alter the consciousness of the people to a point where they cease to ask for a bigger slice of the cake but begin to tackle the real issue, which is the ownership of the bakery. (Burke. B 1999.)

Organic Intellectuals

Gramsci put great emphasis on the crucial role of the intellectual in creating a counter hegemony that would facilitate mass participation instead of depending on an elite group of dedicated revolutionaries, acting for the working class, to bring about an equalitarian society. He asserted that social change had to be the work of the majority of the population conscious of what they were doing and not an organized party leadership and further argued that the revolution led by Lenin and the Bolsheviks in Russia in 1917- which took place in a backward country with a huge peasantry and a tiny working class, and without the involvement of the mass of the population- was not the model suitable for Western Europe or any advanced industrialized country. Mass consciousness and the role of the intellectual were crucial as essential and critical requirements of the counter hegemony strategy.

Gramsci' s definition of intellectuals went far beyond the boffins and academics in ivory towers writing erudite pieces for academic journals only read by others of the same ilk. In his notebooks he writes that "all men (and presumably women) are intellectuals but not all men have in society the function of intellectuals. Everyone at some time fries a couple of eggs or sews up a tear in a jacket; we do not necessarily say that everyone is a cook or a tailor". Meaning that everyone has an intellect and uses it but not all are intellectuals by social function. This is clearly defined in Gramsci's statement that each social group that comes into existence creates within itself one or more strata of intellectuals (managers, civil servants, the clergy, professors and teachers, technicians and scientists, lawyers, doctors etc) that give it meaning, help to bind it together and help it to function. The notion that intellectuals essentially developed organically alongside the rulingclass and function for the benefit of the ruling class shows the notion of intellectuals as being a distinct social category independent of class to be a myth. Gramsci described the traditional intellectuals as those who - despite the fact that they are essentially conservative and allied to and assisting the ruling group in society -regard themselves as autonomous and independent of the dominant social group and are regarded as such by the population at large, and thus give themselves an aura of historical continuity.

This group is constituted of the clergy, the men of letters, the philosophers and professors and others who are traditionally thought of as intellectuals. Gramsci defines organic intellectuals as the group that grows organically within the dominant social group, the ruling class, and is their thinking and organizing element; as a product of the education system, it performs a function for the dominant social group in society and is used by the ruling class to maintain its hegemony over the rest of society.

Gramsci maintained that the requirement for this to happen is not only the cross over of a significant number of 'traditional' intellectuals to the revolutionary cause, as Marx, Lenin and Gramsci had done, but also that the working class movement should produce its own organic intellectuals. Building on his assertion that all individuals (sic) are intellectuals, but not all persons have the function of intellectuals in society, Gramsci posited that "there is no human activity from which every form of intellectual participation can be excluded" and that everyone, outside their particular professional activity, "carries on some form of intellectual activity, participates in a particular conception of the world, has a conscious line of moral conduct, and therefore contributes to sustaining a conception of the world or to modify it, that is, to bring into being new modes of thought".

Even at the risk of being perceived as exaggerating the possibilities, Gramsci was actually trying to stress the fact that people have the capability and the capacity to think, and that the only problem was how to harness those capabilities and capacities. He therefore saw one of his roles (in his capacity as a traditional intellectual, won over to the side of the working class, and therefore transformed into an organic intellectual of the working class) as being that of assisting in the creation of organic intellectuals from the working class and the winning over of as many traditional intellectuals to the revolutionary cause as possible. He attempted to do this through the columns of a journal called L'Ordine Nuovo (New Order), subtitled "a weekly review of Socialist culture".

Gramsci's insistence on the fundamental importance of the ideological struggle to social change meant that this struggle was not limited to consciousness raising but must aim at consciousness transformation - the creation of a socialist consciousness. Arguing that consciousness is not something that could be imposed on people but must arise from their actual working lives, Gramsci propounded the idea that the intellectual realm was not to be seen as something confined to an elite but rather as something grounded in everyday life. [Burke. B 1999.] The creation of working class intellectuals actively participating in practical life, helping to create a counter hegemony that would undermine existing social relations, was Gramsci's contribution to the development of a philosophy that would link theory with practice. This conception ran counter to those elitist and authoritarian philosophies associated with fascism and Stalinism. As Gramsci believed in the innate capacity of human beings to understand their world and to change it, his approach was open and non-sectarian.

Gramsci's ideas on the role of the intellectual are relevant and critical in the discourse on the role of informal educators in local communities, particularly with reference to the notion that the educator working successfully in the neighbourhoods and with the local community has a commitment to that neighbourhood. According to Gramsci-whether s/he may have always lived in the area and have much in common with the local people or not - an organic intellectual/ educator is someone who is not 'here today and gone tomorrow'. On the contrary, organic intellectuals develop relationships with the people they work with and ensure that wherever they go, they are regarded as part of the community. They strive to sustain people's critical commitment to the social groups with whom they share fundamental interests. (Ibid)

The Black Consciousness Movement on ideology and hegemony

The South African Students Organization and the Black People's Convention (SASO/BPC) and a host of socio-political and cultural organizations operating under the rubric of the Black Consciousness Movement - on the ascendancy in South African resistance/liberation politics in the late sixties and early seventies - highlighted the role of (the racist) ideology (of white supremacism) in entrenching the hegemony of the ruling Afrikaner Nationalists, and acknowledged that Apartheid-capitalism thrived not only on coercion and repression but also on the consent of the oppressed black majority. Like Frantz Fanon, Stephen Bantu Biko believed that " the tyranny of the oppressors is prescribed by the endurance of the oppressors." Through the philosophy of Black Consciousness, SASO/BPC emphasized psychological emancipation and mental liberation, self-definition, self-realization, self-awareness, self-reliance and mass conscientisation, mass mobilization and mass participation under the framework of Black Solidarity as a sine qua non for a liberatory culture of resistance/rebellion that would be a counter-hegemony to the hegemony of white supremacism.

Black Consciousness sought to obliterate the myths of white superiority and black inferiority and the normality or the commonsense-ness of the master-servant power-relations between Whites and Blacks/ poor and rich so as to starve white supremacism and racial capitalism of the black inferiority complex and working class compliance/consent upon which Apartheid-capitalism thrived. In the sense that Black Consciousness was -as Donald Woods says-about the mobilization of black opinion against the established White order (Woods A. 1978:149) it could be regarded as a counter- hegemony to white supremacism and racial capitalism. Biko cited the significance and purpose of Black Consciousness and Black Solidarity as helping people to develop some form of security together to look at their problems, and in this way build their humanity. (Woods A. 1978:174). Pronouncing on the conscientisation language and methodology used by the BCM to heighten the revolutionary consciousness necessary for the development of a revolutionary mass of conscious people, Biko declared that SASO/BPC made reference to the conditions of Black people "to get them to grapple realistically with their problems, to attempt to find solutions to their problems, to develop what one might call an awareness of their situation, to be able to provide some kind of hope." (Wood. A 1978:174)

On the role of intellectuals and mass participation

The role of intellectuals (traditional and organic) and the significance of mass participation were eloquently articulated by Stephen Bantu Biko in an interview with Bernard Zylstra in July 1977. Biko asserted that SASO "stressed Black Consciousness and the relations of intellectuals with the needs of the Black community." (Woods. A.1978: 118) He explained that the formation of the Black People's Convention was a result of the realization that - though Black Consciousness had gained momentum -"we were still faced with the practical issue that people who were speaking were mainly students or graduates. There was no broad debate. For this reason we had to move from SASO to the organization of the Black People's Convention so that the masses could get involved in the development of a new consciousness". (Woods. A.1978: 18).Commenting on the successes of the philosophy of Black Consciousness in heightening the revolutionary consciousness that influenced the national students' uprising of 16th June 1976, Biko declared, "the power of a movement lies in the fact that it can indeed change the habits of a people. The change is not the result of force but of dedication, of moral persuasion". (Woods. A.1978: 118).

To Conscientise and enable Black students and graduates (the traditional intellectuals) to establish an organic relationship with the grassroots communities and relate their education / professions to their experiential reality, SASO/ BPC initiated the commemoration of events like the Sharpeville Shooting and initiated commemorative services like "Suffer day", and "Compassion Day". It also established the Black People's Programmes, embarking on a variety of educational, awareness and self-help community development projects ranging from health clinics, literacy programmes, and poetry groups to cooperatives. The purpose of these initiatives was explained clearly by Stephen Bantu Biko in the SASO/BPC trial: "Compassion day was meant for remembrance of specific situations of affliction that the Black man was subjected to from time to time, things like starvation in places like Dimbaza, things like floods in Port Elizabeth…. The main idea of compassion day was to get students to develop a social conscience, to see themselves as a part of the communities, and direct their energies to solving problems of the nature we were thinking about on compassion day." (Woods. A 1978:160-161)

This relationship between theory and practice, education and experiential reality, knowledge and social reality, informed the conceptualization, design and implementation of the programmes of the Black Consciousness Movement. This comes out clearly in Biko's account of the research he, Jerry Modisane and Barney Pityana conducted in the preparation of the literacy program that was drawn up by SASO. They listened to women in queues waiting to see a doctor or nurse at a clinic –some carrying babies on their backs, to people in shebeens and to people in buses and trains. In all these situations-Biko observed- there was a constant occurrence of "protest talk" about the general conditions of oppression and exploitation, such as the de-humanizing and denigrating impact of the migratory labour and single hostels system, exploitative labour practices and unsafe and unhealthy working and living conditions. He outlined that their aim and purpose with the research was to familiarize themselves with the generic terms that the people in the target area were familiar with and to get in touch with the people's day-to-day experiences, concerns and issues and their perception and conception of these issues.

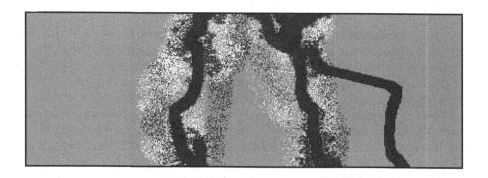

Biko's presentation and articulation of the whole process is instructive: "… this particular method we were using placed a lot of emphasis on syllabic teaching of people. You did not just teach people the alphabet in isolation, you had to teach them syllables, and you had to start with words that had a particular meaning to them, what we called generative terms. Now the preamble to it was some kind of research in the specific area in which you were going to work, which carried you to several segments of the community, to particular places where the community congregated and talked freely. Your role there was particularly passive. You were just there to listen to the things they were talking about, and also to the words that were being used. We also used pictures to depict the themes they were talking about."(Woods. A.1978: 172)

Here it is lucidly clear that the BCM saw literacy as not merely being lettered and numerate or being able to read and write alphabets and count numbers but also as the ability to read one's world /environment and (re)write one's reality/ history; in other words - being socio-politically literate and culturally aware. Literacy and education were perceived as tools that capacitate a person to critically and constructively grapple with natural and social phenomena and to actively interact and engage with his/ her natural and social surroundings. The literacy programmes, political education programmes (mass rallies and political workshops or initiation schools -in SASO/BPC parlance-) together with the self-help cooperatives and political campaigns were part of a single and integrated strategy to move the Black Person from social experience to consciousness to social action to the changing of social experience.

Biko and the BCM on revolutionary transformation

It is noteworthy that for Biko and the BCM the point was no longer to reform the system, as doing so would imply the acceptance of the basic precepts around which the system evolved but to completely overhaul it. Therefore the BCM castigated Gatsha Buthelezi and other Bantustan leaders and later participants in the sham trichameral parliament and the dummy Black Local Authority councils for –in the words of Steve Biko-diluting the cause by operating on government platforms. The BCM shunned attempting to change the system from within as many reformists-sometimes evoking Gramsci- sought to do. As a result the BCM placed emphasis on the principle of non-collaboration with the ruling class and its political instruments. It presented Black Solidarity and Black Power as the real force that will bring about seizure of power to prepare for a revolutionary transformation of society. While acknowledging that the BCM under the leadership of SASO/BPC was not yet at a stage to present the details of the alternative system, Biko highlighted that the BCM recognized the fact that "a change in the colour of the occupier does not necessarily change the system", and also acknowledged that "the debate about economic policy cannot be "pure", completely separate from existing systems."   (Biko cited in Woods. A 1978:122)

In its search for an alternative to Apartheid-Capitalism, SASO/ BPC identified consultation, communalism and public ownership of the land as the basic precepts and tenets of the agrarian economic system that prevailed in the rudimentary culture of traditional, pre-colonial African society and sought to appropriate these to develop a more expounded (?} economic system accommodating industry and the relationship of industry and politics. Hence the BCM under SASO/ BPC initially spoke about Black communalism and collective enterprise and started discussions around what Stephen Bantu Biko referred to as "socialist solution that is an authentic expression of Black communalism." (Biko cited in Woods. A 1978:122)

By the late seventies and early eighties, Black Consciousness formations like the Azanian People's Organization, Azanian Students' Movement and later the Azanian Students' Convention and the Azanian Youth Organization were overtly talking of scientific socialism as their official ideology.   The post-apartheid South Africa saw the emergence of the Socialist Party of Azania articulating a more vociferously socialistic expression of Black Consciousness and affiliated to the International Liasons Committee of Workers and Peoples / Fourth International.

REFERENCES

1. Boggs, C. (1976) Gramsci's Marxism. London: Pluto Press
2. Burke, B. (1999) 'Antonio Gramsci and informal education', the encyclopaedia of informal education, http://www.infed.org\thinkers\et-gram.htm
3. Gramsci, A. (1971). Selections from the Prison Notebooks. London: Lawrence and Wishart
4. Woods. A. 1978. Biko-The true story of the young South African martyr and his struggle to raise Black Consciousness. New York: Henry Holt and Company. Inc

CULTURE & LIBERATION: Steve and Strini sang from the same songbook as Fanon

"My spirit sits in shell of my palm/ and the embryo slowly forms/ nestling in the warmth/ of the embryonic fluid/ I watch myself change/ the slow development/ my birth has come in my life…..Slowly my soul moves/ towards the mapped out destiny / And smiling it advances…"
- *An excerpt from "Revolution in Conception"*, a poem by Strini Moodley

Professor Ben Khoapa's presentation on "Fanon and the psychology of Oppression" at the recent discussion forum hosted by Umtapo Center focused on Fanon's perspective that the development of a national culture is inseparable from the struggle for liberation and socio-economic-political transformation, and that the issue of identity is connected to the question of oppression or liberation. In his preliminary remarks to the talk, Khoapa referred to the genocidal attacks on the civilians in Lebanon and Palestine and the world's double standards, and also made reference to increased socio-economic disparities in South Africa. He specifically lamented the fact that former freedom strugglers seem more comfortable with the prospective of South Africa becoming a country of 10 millionaires and 45 million impoverished people and less concerned about renaming the country Azania. He asserted that the latter would be an act of breaking with colonial history and of reasserting the right of a people to name and define themselves and to develop their own culture and identity. The presentation sparked a lively discussion on the relevancy of Fanon's views on the relationship between the development of a national culture and the politics of liberation and resistance in the current era of global capitalism and in view of the devastating consequences of neo-liberalism on local communities. It once again vindicated the continued relevance of a Black Consciousness discourse that puts emphasis on the relationship between psychological emancipation/mental liberation and physical liberation and the importance of culture in the struggle for liberation.

It is not incidental that the military invasions on the peoples of the South by American Imperialism in the era of the cold war were euphemistically referred to as the culture wars and that the genocidal attacks on the peoples of the Middle East in the post-war dispensation are posited by bourgeoisie scholars as being a part of the clash of civilizations. All forms of oppression, exploitation, discrimination and denigration of a people and of unequal allocation of power and inequitable distribution of wealth and resources thrive on and perpetuate the denial of the humanity of a people, the commoditization of their labor, the plunder of their land and the denigration of their history, culture and way of life. All forms of oppression and exploitation sustain themselves by perpetuating the myth and lie that the oppressed and exploited people have no history, culture and civilization, and that it is to their benefit that they live under thesubjugation and tutelage of the exploiter class, oppressor nation and/or colonizing/occupying force. Imperialism, colonialism, racism, Zionism and related forms of oppression and discrimination thrive on the de-personalization, objectification, de-humanization of the other and the valorization or vulgarization of their way of life\culture and the depiction of their land as a virgin territory prior to the arrival of the colonizing and occupying nation/culture/civilization. Crude metaphors like "dark continent" and "land without people for a people without land," have been used to deny Africans and Palestinians any sense of history, culture, civilization and identity other than the one carved out for them by imperialist and colonial history.

Those who rebel and seek to define themselves and to take control of their lives are depicted as rebellious brutes and those who live within the confines of the culture of the masters are rated as being civilized and cultured. Those who opt for art for art's sake, literature for pleasure's sake and the divorcing of culture from political and socio-economic concerns are celebrated as mature. And the literary and aesthetic value of the proponents of art with a social conscience, the literature of commitment and the culture of resistance is questioned. This is because a culture rooted in social experience and relevant to the historical-material realities of a people, gives people a sense of where they come from, how they arrived where they are, and how they can move forward to a better future. But a culture detached from social experience and historical-material realities breeds an uncritical and unconscious mass of people who make no connection between the relations of the forces of production, power relations in society and the culture of a people.

The truth of the matter is that a people's way of living is informed by and dictated to by the way a society's economy is structured and by the power relations in that specific society. A people that do not control their natural resources and their major means of production and have no political power at their disposal cannot hope to be in control of how they live their lives. Even if they have some idea of their historical-cultural heritage, a people without economic and political power lack the material and intellectual resources and political authority required to develop a culture informed by their historical experiences and material realities, and to carve out for themselves an identity not made in the image of others. A simple example: according to the culture of the indigenous people of Azania, a person has to be buried where his/her umbilical cord lies. But today many rural and urban Africans are not able to do so even if they wish and desire to do so, because they are a landless people.

This highlights the bitter reality that a people without land, economic and political power are a people without culture. In a capitalist, neo-colonial country like ours, profit accumulation, consumerism and materialism have taken over the people's culture. The dominant values paraded in the private and public media and in movies, plays and books are those of individualism, consumerism, materialism and Americanism. The continued political and economic marginalization of the masses of poor working class people translates itself into the cultural hegemony of a Euro-centric, elitist culture and the cultural marginalization of Black people and the working class. Whatever remnants of their historical-cultural heritage remain, are suffocated by the trappings of capital. The point we are making here is hat one can never build a humanist egalitarian peoples' culture without transforming a society dominated by a capitalist bourgeoisie into an egalitarian one. On the other hand, one cannot hope to build an egalitarian society without inculcating humane, communalistic, communitarian, Ubuntu ethics and values into the people and without employing the history and the remaining positive and constructive aspects of the culture of a people as a resource and a tool of resistance, struggle and transformation. But the elements of the historical-cultural heritage of a people that remain have to be inserted into the current and daily experiences of a people and be connected to the contemporary local and global struggles of the wretched of the earth for them to have a libratory cultural value.

The crux of the matter here is that culture has to give people the identity of a free and liberated people. Denying a people an identity is central to the denial of their humanity, and therefore the vilification of their way of life and their knowledge-and-belief system is an integral part of the process of colonization and occupation. To deny a person an identity and a sense of being and belonging is basically to deny him freedom; and slavery basically entails being denied an identity or a sense of being and belonging. Freedom struggles and wars of liberation are ultimately about asserting the right of a people to be and to belong, which invariably means the right to define oneself and one's world, the right to regulate one's social, political, economic and personal conduct and the right of a people to their collective power and the resources accrued from their land for their survival according to the terms and values laid down by them. Hence, Fanon is spot on whenhe argues that culture without resistance to oppression or rather culture without liberation is culture without substance. Culture must help to restore and preserve the personhood, humanity and humanness of a people and protect their inalienable right to be and belong.

Culture must give people identity, dignity and freedom. There is no culture and no identity for an un-free people. A people can only develop a culture worth its salt if the development of that culture is a part of the libratory project. Culture is usually defined as the way of life in a given society and the sum total of the spiritual and material achievements of a society. This includes a society's knowledge-and-belief-system, norm-and-value system; customs and traditions, folklore, legends and myths; artifacts and architecture, and the oral, literary, visual and performing arts. These provide a people with stories, symbols, heroines/heroes, models, dreams, and visions that are a narrative of their past/ history, a reflection and analysis of the present and, by providing a window into their tomorrow, an exploration of the future.

In this sense, culture is a medium that relates the past and the history of a people, a tool for them to grapple with the present and material realities and a force that spurs them towards the future and fuels them with a hope for a new tomorrow- built out of the mosaic of their historical-material, socio-cultural and politico-economic experiences. By giving a people a sense of their past, an understanding of their present and a vision for the future, culture accords people the right and responsibility to define and redefine themselves and their world, to remember, re-member and re-construct the past with the view of taking control of the present and of re-organizing their world in order to shape and define their future. In other ways, culture gives a people a sense of being and belonging and reaffirms, restores and reclaims their humanity/identity. Therefore culture is essentially about liberation, freedom and resistance. This is because the foundational principle of all forms of oppression, exploitation, discrimination, de-humanization and brutalization (imperialism, capitalism, colonialism, racism, xenophobia, tribalism, sexism, able-ism, etc) is the denial of the humanity, and therefore of the identity of oppressed other. All forms of oppression are based on and result in the de-personalization/de-humanization, objectification of a people and valorization/vulgarization of their culture.

It is easy to see why imperialism and colonialism aim to annihilate the culture of a people they seek to oppress and exploit. Culture is the product of human interaction with the natural and social environment and the result of the exploration and utilization of natural and social laws for survival. It captures the historical- material experiences of a people and articulates shared social, economic and political conditions and experiences. At the same time culture provides for individuated, innovative and imaginative expressions of historical-material conditions/socio-economic and political experiences, and allows for an articulation of the personal voice and an expression of personal experiences in both the private and public spheres of life. In essence the notion of the dichotomy between the private and public spheres and the compartmentalization of knowledge was unknown in the cultures of pre-capitalist communalistic/ communitarian/societies.Culture is grounded in the interconnectedness between various facets and aspects of life. It is informed by and reflects the interrelationship between the natural and social world, the material and spiritual or physical and metaphysical realms of life, and between the psychosocial and politico-economic wellbeing of society. African culture in particular advances the idea of the timelessness of time and the relativity of space, as well as the notion of the past-present-future and body-mind-soul-spirit continuum. It is rooted in the notion of the interconnectness of the worlds and the interconnectness of humanity and the oneness of the peoples of the world.

Thus culture in itself is antithetical to the idea of dividing the peoples of the world along artificial and arbitrary boundaries, and asserts, "You are because I am, and I am because you are," Motho ke Motho ka Batho". But this is not the monopoly of African culture. It is not something written in the DNA of a particular creed of a particular people. The culture of Ubuntu/pro-humanism is the product of a socio-economic-political system based on the equitable and just allocation of resources and participatory modes of governance, and the erosion of its values by individualistic and materialistic ethos is a product of a system based on an inequitable and unjust allocation of power and resources and on the systematic plunder of the wealth and cultures of the peoples of the Global South by the imperialistic countries of the Global North. To reclaim the culture of humanity therefore necessitates the transformation and reconstruction of the unequal power relations and inequitable distribution of wealth and resources and the ushering in of a society based on justice, equity and equality. For as long as the economic disparities continue and for as long as the remnants of Apartheid-Capitalism are not removed, the reclamation of a humane, humanist and egalitarian culture will remain an illusive dream. Frantz Fanon was not alone in arguing the case of culture as a weapon of struggle. The founding fathers of the Black Consciousness Movement in Azania like Steve Biko (the first president of SASO/BPC) and Strini Moodley (Biko's associate and the founder of the first Union of Black theatre) knew that their dream of a South Africa with a human face would not materialize until the culture of an oppressed people became the culture of resistance and until the aim of culture was to liberate the minds of the oppressed from the mental chains and to liberate their labor from the claws of capital. Therefore, the emergence of the Black Consciousness Movement led to a resurgence of resistance arts and Black theology. Black people started to relate their cultural practices and artistic expressions to their daily experiences and also began to explore for ways and means of relating the text of religious scriptures to their everyday reality. Students asked themselves whether what they learned in classrooms related to the reality they experienced in the streets, factories, slums and pondokies, and sought for ways of unlearning in the school of real life what they learned in the bourgeois institution.

When Steve Biko was asked to point out the success of this psychological, socio-political and cultural reawakening, he answered with one word:" Soweto". He was referring to the national students uprising of 16 June 1976. Thirty years after the youth uprising, the country is a morass of moral degeneration. Incidents of abuse and molestation of women are on the rise, the levels of crime, poverty and inequality have escalated and hardly a day passes without a story of a public servant or Member of Parliament being involved in act of corruption.

Communities have not been able to organize themselves to be able to effectively and efficiently address these challenges. People are calling for a moral regeneration and a cultural reclamation as one of the strategies to deal with the problems of HIV/AIDS, crime, corruption, poverty and inequality.

But culture does not exist in a vacuum. The womb within which culture is born is the historical and material conditions and the prevailing socio-economic and political system. How is it possible to inculcate humanistic and communalistic values within the framework of a neo-capitalist, neo-liberal system? Can we realistically call for moral regeneration and cultural reclamation without calling for the scrapping of GEAR and the halting of our country's march towards unbridled capitalism, state withdrawal and the rule of the market? What would Stephen Bantu Bikoand Strinivasa Strini Moodley, have said in this context? It will need another paper, if not a book to elucidate how the theme of the relationship between psychological and cultural emancipation and socio-economic and political freedom resonates and runs like a thread through the plays, poems and speeches of comrade Strini and in the writings of comrade Steve Biko. It will demand another book to look at how in their political and social conduct Steve and Strini actualized this. But I want to believe that as they did under Apartheid-Capitalism, Steve and Strini would, under neo-colonial, neo-capitalist, neo-liberal South Africa have argued for a linkage between culture and the way in which the economy of a society is organized.

I want to believe they would have acknowledged the connection between a people's way of life and the relationship between the forces of production. I believe they would have located the quest for an African Renaissance within the framework of the struggle to break with imperialism/ global capitalism and would have called upon Africa and the world to ditch the Washington Consensus, and for South Africa to throw the reverse GEAR into the dustbins where it belongs. I further believe that this country and the world stand to benefit a lot from the writings, teachings and actions of Bantu Biko and Strini Moodley and their disciples, as far as the use of culture as a libratory tool of resistance, awareness-raising and social transformation is concerned.

THE MYTH OF TWO ECONOMIES

The sudden preoccupation of South African politicians, analysts, commentators -and even a handful of activists- with the idea that the problem of South Africa is mainly that of the existence of **two economies,** is a typical example of how the use of **plastic concepts** and **euphemisms** to hide the failures of the system, can become an effective tool in the hands of the establishment.

Having ditched the Reconstruction and Development Programme for the Growth and Redistribution (GEAR) policy, the government is faced with the glaring reality that **GEAR** and **BEE** have delivered maximum profits for Big Capital and economic opportunities for the Black elites and their White partners but almost 'zilch' to the poorest of the poor. Through the poetic genius of president Thabo **"The bard"** Mbeki, the neo-liberal regime is now churning out useful metaphors and nice-sounding dictums like "**two economies**" and **"shared growth."** The truth of the matter is that economic policies based on **trickle-down** logic cannot be relied on for equitable and just distribution and allocation of power and resources.

The emphasis of the Growth and Redistribution **(GEAR)** project on economic growth was based on the belief that the benefits of the growth would slowly but surely trickle down to the poorest of the poor in the form of job creation and opportunities for informal businesses and small and medium enterprises. But now we know that the season of boom for the markets does not necessarily translate itself into jobs and opportunities for the poor and marginalized. Deregulation and privatization and downsizing and rightsizing have resulted in the loss of more and more jobs in both the public and private sector. Water and electricity cut-offs and evictions have outnumbered the number of houses that were built as well as the number of homes that got water and electricity. The new houses are nothing more than concrete slabs and most of the **'new townships'** are glorified squatter camps, with no clinics, schools, libraries, and other social amenities and cultural centres. More students are finding it difficult to access tertiary education. Those who have made it to universities and Technikons are hugely in debt and have only a slim chance of finding a job. The world of business continues to be inaccessible to the poorest of the poor. The small farmers, informal tradesmen, hawkers, artisans and artists, not to mention the women, continue to battle to eke a living for themselves and to build a future for their children. The disparities between White and Black, poor and rich, and low, middle and high-income earners continue to widen every day.

Suddenly the government has woken up and has started talking about the need for **shared growth.** It blames the situation on the existence of two economies and continually harps on the need to invest more in the second economy. By **the first economy** it refers to **Big Capital.** By the second economy, the government seems to refer to the small and medium enterprises and the people involved in the so-called informal trade: people involved in spaza shops, small hair-salons, shebeens and stokvels and small taxi owners, as well as the "street artisans", tailors, hawkers and low-scale subsistence farmers. It says the major challenge is to grow the first economy and then use the spin-offs thereof to invest in the second economy.

As it is often the case with government-speak, this is nothing more than an obscurantist escape from the world of social reality to the world of euphemisms. To speak of **two economies** is to side-step and evade the reality that non-racial, neo-liberal, capitalist South Africa has failed the litmus test of addressing the imbalances and inequities created by **Apartheid-Capitalism,** and has actually broadened the enormous chasm that already existed between the rich and the poor, between labourers and managers and between low-income and high-income earners. The fact of the matter is that we have one **market-driven economy** in which a tiny and minute section of the population is active and finds itself filthy rich, whilst the majority of the population struggles to get its slice of bread, and is told to go for cake-crumbs.

Most of the people who are said to be involved in the so-called **second economy** are basically part and parcel of the **subaltern people** who find themselves at the margins of the **market economy.** Simply put, the second economy is a euphemism for people on the fringes of the market economy. To put it in another way the periphery within the market economy has been re-defined as the **second economy.** The bulk of the people we are speaking about, when we euphemistically talk of **the second economy,** come from communities that are forever battling against unemployment and escalating levels of crime and moral degeneration, harshly affecting people who receive the short end of the global capitalist stick.

These are communities that are killed daily by diseases mostly associated with the conditions of poverty and squalor and HIV/AIDS, and for whom literacy, quality education, quality health services, decent housing and fully equipped social amenities are rare commodities. These people do not have the luxury of hefty salaries and car and housing allowances. They have a slim chance of getting business loans from formal institutions of finance that still look at Black working class people - and poor people in general - with distrust and suspicion. They have little economic and political clout to get them government tenders and **BEE** deals that depend heavily on the new Mzansi currency known as **"political connectivity."**

To ameliorate the conditions of these people necessitates an acknowledgement of the structural nature of poverty and inequality in order to deal honestly with the legacy of Apartheid-capitalism and the devastation caused by neo-liberal policies on the poor communities. This requires a commitment to scrap **GEAR** and introduce policies that will begin to prioritize the welfare and wellbeing of society and the environment rather than subject the country to the demon of profit and the god of economic growth. We can only begin to move in this direction when we start acknowledging the inequitable nature of the **market economy** rather than put our heads in the sand like ostriches and hide behind the security of euphemisms and myths such as **the two economies.**

BLACK CONSCIOUSNESS UNBUNDLED

Black Consciousness as a response to the politics of Race and Class

The philosophy of Black Consciousness is distinguished from narrow nationalist ideologies and a-historic expressions of the socialist ideology, by its fusion of the class and national question and the contextualization of the ideology of socialism to the Azanian situation of settler-colonialism and racial-capitalism, and neocolonial and neoliberal capitalism. As a dialectic response of the Black working class to settler-colonial racial-capitalism, and neocolonial, neoliberal capitalism as it exists in Azania today, Black Consciousness is a synthesis of the theories of various socialist and nationalist thinkers and writers- Marx, Engels, Lenin, Mao, Trotsky; Fanon, Cabral, Cesaire, Malcolm X etc - to the historical-material realities of Azania.

Basically, socialists struggle for a society wherein power and resources are equitably distributed through the socialization of land, state control and public ownership of the major means of production and the active participation of the workers and broader society in decision-making and policy formulation. For this to be realized socialists do not rely on chance and conjecture, guesswork and mystery, but on a revolutionary theory and revolutionary practice called Scientific Socialism. Its tools of analysis are Historical Materialism and Dialectic-Materialism, which assert that social phenomena are not accidental but a product of historical events which are themselves products of human beings' engagement with the world, and therefore that human beings are not passive products of history but rather makers of history. But people do not write history or social change on a blank page. Historical-material conditions, existential and experiential realities and contextual circumstances inform their actions. Hence Karl Marx asserted that it is not the consciousness of a people that determines their material conditions but rather the material conditions of a people that determine their consciousness. The logic of historical and dialectic materialism dictates that a philosophy /ideology should have a historical specificity and be informed by concrete and tangible material realities and empiric socio-economic-political conditions.

Born out of the womb of, and as an antithesis to settler-colonialism, apartheid-capitalism and liberalism, Black Consciousness is rooted in the historical-material realities and socio-economic-political conditions of the working and underclasses of Azania- who for obvious reasons are predominately Black. It articulates mental and psychological liberation as a way of breaking free from a false consciousness and a false identity imposed on the working and underclasses by social stratification along class and colour lines. It goes on to present self-realization, self-awareness, group politics and the solidarity of Black people with the working and underclasses and oppressed people of the world, as the bedrock for national self-determination and the seizure of socio-economic-political power by the poor and working classes. This fusion of the Black Consciousness philosophy with socialist ideology is a dialectical and revolutionary response and the antithesis to the marriage of class exploitation and racial discrimination under settler-colonial apartheid-capitalism, and neocolonial, neoliberal capitalism as it exists in Azania today.

Black Consciousness as a response to the colonial divide and rule strategy

Whatever its shades, colonialism begins with words in people's minds. This means that colonialism involves a discursive process of controlling a people's self-definition and understanding of themselves and the world around them. It uses social stratification, the skewed and racial allocation of power and resources, and linguistic and cultural hegemony to dictate a particular world-view and conceptualization of social reality to a people, and thus imposes a false consciousness and a false identity on them. By a false identity we refer to an identity that is not informed by a people's historical-material realities and socio-economic-political conditions, but is carved out for them by officialdom, the corporate media and mass culture.

For example, the people of Rwanda speak one language, Kinyarwanda. As language is a carrier of a people's historical-cultural heritage, this means that they share one historical-cultural heritage and have one knowledge-and-belief system and one norm-and-value system. But when the Belgians colonised that country, they came up with a social classification system whereby everyone and anyone who had ten cows was classified as a Tutsi, everybody having less than ten, but up to five cows was called a Hutu and those who had fewer cows were Mutwa. In their identity documents these class divisions were recorded as "races". So what began as a social stratification system imposed by the colonialists was systemically codified into artificial tribal divisions, where before there had been no tribes but one people. These were the roots of the genocide of 1994 where one million people were killed in a hundred days.

In Azania the apartheid regime arbitrarily imposed the terms Kaffir, Bantu, Native, Boeseman, Coloured, Coolie on Black people of indigenous African origin, Black people of Khoisan and Malay origins and Black people of Asian or India-Pakistani origin. They went further and associated these "labels" with derogatory, de-humanizing, degrading and denigrating stereotypes about Black people. Through this they systematically instilled in Black people an inferiority complex that made them ashamed of their blackness to the extent of venerating whiteness and aspiring to be White, because as Frantz Fanon articulated it in "Black Skins; White Masks": *"My body was given back to me sprawled out; distorted, re-colored, clad mourning... The Negro is an animal, the Negro is ugly; look, a nigger, it's cold, the nigger is...cold the little black boy is trembling because he is afraid of the nigger..."* Furthermore, they created socio-economic-political inequities, boundaries and barriers that served to entrench these stereotypes and myths.

The socio-economic conditions of poverty and squalor in varying degrees served not only to brutalize Black people into self-shame and self-hate, but to also set the different sections of the Black Community against each other. It was a divide-and-rule strategy to act as a bulwark against Black people of diverse origins, preventing them from uniting around common problems and issues and shared aspirations and needs. It is in this context that the Black Consciousness Movement initiated what Biko referred to *"as an inward-looking process of self-definition."* This meant that we had to define ourselves on the basis of shared socio-economic and political conditions and historical-material experiences.

We found that irrespective of whether we were of India-Pakistani, Malay-Khoisan origins or of a so-called "non-racial" parentage,(?) we were economically excluded from owning the major means of production and productive land, as well as politically excluded from universal adult suffrage and socially degraded. Therefore we agreed on Black as a political term referring to everybody who was psychologically oppressed, economically exploited, politically discriminated against and socially denigrated by Apartheid-Capitalism. Paradoxically speaking, "Black" included all people anywhere in the world who shared the conditions of being by law or tradition, psychologically exploited, economically oppressed, politically discriminated against, and socially degraded…be it in Palestine, United States, Brazil or Australia.

Black Consciousness and the politics of identity and self-determination

It was imperative that an oppressed people in search of liberation should define and name themselves, because naming is an expression of power and authority and a political act. When a person defines and names a thing he or she actually exercises power and authority over that thing. The definer and namer define the reality of the named and shape its very being and destiny. To be defined and named by the other or take on the identity and consciousness carved out for you by another is to be robbed of a sense of identity. To be denied a sense of self-identity is to be denied a sense of being and belonging. No one can be free as long as he or she is made in the image of someone else.

So, the process of self-definition and self-naming is the first step towards consciousness, consciousness is the activator of action, and action is the shaper and re-shaper of one's reality, experience, and destiny. As Biko taught us, you cannot be conscious and remain inactive. Consciousness should steer you to action, and action should be aimed at movement and change.

This is what the Black Consciousness Movement meant- moving from experience to consciousness, to action, to the changing of experience. One's conditions, experiences, realities, situation, environment, and context inform the process of self-definition and self-awareness, self-reliance and self-assertiveness. Self-consciousness, self-reliance and self-assertiveness lead to independent, creative, ingenious, and innovative action and action brings about change. But here we are talking of the collective self-consciousness of a people, social action and social change. Why is the exercise of self-identity and self-definition so important for people fighting slavery, colonialism and imperialism? Slavery and colonialism in their varying forms were not only geared to exploiting Black people economically, but were also aimed at reshaping their reality, so that they became willing slaves and willing servants. For instance, in Azania the system was geared to making the demands of Apartheid the cornerstone of the Black People's reality so that fulfilment for them would mean filling the role into which the philosophy of colonialism had moulded them. In other words, Black people had to confirm the white man's stereotypes about them and not question the white man's assertions and supposed sacrosanct authority. Therefore the black person was not portrayed as a human being but depicted as a "type".

As a type the Black person could either be a good nigger (fulfilling the role assigned to him /her by white authority) or a rebellious incarnation of evil that the White world is justified in isolating and crushing with the arsenal of public information and state machinery at its disposal. *(See Mazisi Kunene's introduction to Aime Cesaire's "Return to My Native Land", published by Penguin Books in 1969).* Black Consciousness is the re-humanization of a historically dispossessed de-humanized and brutalized people. A dispossessed person is a de-personalized and de-socialized being because a person without land cannot have the economic and political power without which one has no history and culture to speak of nor a sense of being and belonging and a sense of dignity and worth. This is succinctly illustrated in the famous answer of the father whose son inquired why all tales ended with the lion being vanquished, and wanted to know why there is no single recorded victory of the king of the jungle. The old man answered that unless and until the lion learns to write its own stories and tells its own tales; there will be no story in which it appears as the victor. This answer eloquently captures the stance of Black Consciousness: Black People should be the objects, subjects and agents of their own liberation and determine their own destiny; then they will be able to write their own history and decide their own future.

But Black Consciousness argues that only those who possess power and resources can control the process of the generation, accumulation and dissemination of knowledge and information and therefore dictate how history is written and how society is organized economically, socially, politically and culturally. And that political power accrues from economic power, which is derived from ownership and control of the land and its wealth and resources. Therefore Black Consciousness is about the return of the land to people (in this case, Black People) and of the people back to themselves. It is the call for Black People to be and remain themselves rather than be appendages of other people or additional levers in the capitalist machine. That can only be a reality when Black people control the economy of the country and are not just in political office. For Black Consciousness political power minus economic power is not enough. The purpose of seizing political power is to use that power as leverage to bring about economic transformation aimed at equitable redistribution of the wealth and resources of the land and ensure that the needs and aspirations of the working class are held paramount. Black Consciousness is much more relevant in Azania today because, as Lybon Tiyani Mabasa correctly observed at the SOPA Congress in 2003: *"White dominance continues unabated in all avenues of life, continuously reinforcing the stereotype that Black people are inferior and therefore incapable."* (See The Truth. No 35 December 2003:89-92)

Paper presented at the Wentworth Youth Political Development Workshop hosted by the Wentworth Development Forum –12-14 July 2004

ON BOARD THE 'SCAMTHO TRAIN WITH BRA IKE

BOOK: Gova
WRITER: Ike Mboneni Muila
ISBN: 0-620-31395-1
PUBLISHER: Botsotso Publishing

Way back in the days of the Kofifi of "ons daak nie, ons phola hierso", when the line of demarcation between the mogoe and the clever was as succinctly clear as mud, the jietas and cherries would say "Do not talk the talk if you cannot walk the walk." That was to say that the ghetto lingua franca that is Iscamtho, the so-called Tsotsi Taal is more than a lingo but a lifestyle, born out of the concrete and tangible historical-material experiences of a people living the nightmare of Apartheid-Capitalism, aka Separate Development. Nowadays Iscamtho, the township way, is on the television and even the market communicates via the witty lingo to seduce the masses to embrace the new religion called consumerism. And so the Roccobarocco advertorial might be something like: *"Dimmer joe/ shwele baba/ shwele nkosiyami/ ama dimmers line/ vole verse open and close chapter page edlawathi gazi/ hola seven/ with Roccobarocco spectacles and sunglasses design/ bly jy 'n ou manotcher/ skuvert under corset …"*

Not to be outshined by Roccobarocco, the spin doctors for Doom might chant and portray it as a macho Rambo running amok on bed bugs and other uninvited guests in our kitchen units: *"super doom rambo/ ungu mhlobo wenene emakhayeni wethu/ super doom Rambo/ thanyela i cockroach/ imbizo ya maphela nembovane/ time and again stray ratas/ careless uninvited crawling insect/ bed bucks of no particular origin/ super doom rambo shosholo/ i mosquito rumba dance ngolovane/ jive gate crushing in our kitchen unit…"* But this is not the voice over the tell-lie-vision screen. It is the tongue-in-cheek groot bek of Mboneni Wangu Muila, word-wand and master minder of all the official and unofficial languages of South Africa - *"the languages of humour and hope and horror-the languages of love and listlessness-the languages of poetry and passion and putrefaction."*

With his roots in the Northern Province of Limpopo in Venda via the Zambezi River, Mboneni Wangu Muila was born in nineteen ou dubula matsetse in the year of bed bucks suckers at a Mofolo village - where his parents settled after forced removal from Sophiatown. And Ike - he says in "Autobiography"- is his *"Venda name colonized and sodomized by the anglo sex language with empty promises of heaven on earth".*

From being a newspaper street vendor boy mgobozi, wearing an Iwisa maize mealie-meal-bag t-shirt and green line shorts with no dirty dozen under his rough cast concrete feet called mukenke crocodile skin cracks, to suffering multiple failures at Vista University in Dlamini in Soweto, attempting a BA degree in Education, Ike attended the Masechaba High Open-Ended University of Experience and entered the world of creative writing as a poet-artist-performer. His flight dream came true when he literally shat in the air on a trip to Berlin in Germany on the way to a poetry conference held under the title zungeschlag…slip of a tongue. Against the history of the domination of South Africa by imperial (European and North American) cultures and the current wave of bombardment by Rap and pseudo-Rasta speak, Ike Mboneni Wangu Muila - 'the international minister of foreign affairs' from *"South Africa, the world in one country"* oozes *"ringas spitting words undilutable bile"*.

The result is Gova - a language Movement behind a Black Moses and a definitive guide to the poetics of the slanguage and lingua franca of Township South Africa —Iscamtho, Ringas, Ghetto Lingo, so-called Tsotsi Taal - and a commentary on the socio-economic and cultural experiences that informs it. From the word go, this witty lingo eliminates tribal divisions and xenophobia and resonates with the spirit of Ubuntu and unity in diversity, fusing all the spoken languages together to greet all the inhabitants of Msawawa:

> *"Mangwanani/ Sanibonani/ thobela/ re ya losha*
> *Welele ebukhosini/ bakhiwa hola/ sharp hoezit moja*
> *To my dear friends/ brothers and sisters at heart*
> *Assalaam alaikom/ Alaikom salaam."*

The full stop is preceded by a prayer for the Good Lord to save the Queen from insinuating a war monger beast in that bush of the United States of America, as *"both Americans juju monkey do monkey see".*

This is followed by a deliberate subversion of the grammatical and literary rules and conventions of the English language in the narrative celebration of Isabella Motadinyane, an avant garde, free spirited poet who died of ulcer complications resulting from her tubes being blocked after her mother took her *"to a family planning clinic for a sterile and birth control while she was a young school girl for fear of unwanted pregnancy".* Using street English-cum-everyday speak —cum-real life-lingo Muila recalls: : *" she wrote a poem that gave birth to botsotso publishing and botsotso poetry performers as botsotso jesters I met isabella while a stage manager for their workshop play about life in theatre pimville of the early sixties of gangsterism, music and social politics of that time even in the tsotsi taal lingo in particular times under the title skom short for skom plaas that is emzini… during tea time andlunch time we would be discussing creative writing that is poetry and state drama performance complementing each other she became my soul mate and she told me to throw away my walking stick which I used to keep my body up straight while struggling with the force of gravity since my permanent brain fracture blow I suffered in 91 jeppe street jozi, i wrote her a poem my better half."*

111.

The emotive flow of words and beautiful mix of poetic, prosaic, journalistic, narrative and dramatic register is typical of the late 70's writers of the calibre of Muthobi Motloatse, who coined the term Proemdra Prose, poetry, music and drama all rolled into one. Here Muila takes readers into the world of two poets confronting their traumatic and testing physical-psycho-social conditions through mutual support, mutual love and the weapon and therapy of humour and the spoken word. He shares with readers how Isabella would curl up in bed with the squeaky sounds of "echu"-an exclamation of pain in Sesotho… and a fart followed by a hysterical laugh and an explanation to him that the pain is gone with the fart:

"I would hold and kiss her and then ask her what she would love to drink before and after the meal as a wash down and she would tell me she is tired of drinking white waters that is milk sugar and hot water as her one and only tea she would love to drink beer and be merry wayawaya to entertain the mass of poetry lovers with beer in one hand drinking like nobody's business and with our creative writing coming home with raving reviews I could easily remember vividly she creatively wrote sink and shaft before a beer bottle while we were rehearsing poetry and spontaneously collectively creating and recreating folk songs that would go along with the poetry in Grahamstown poetry festival performance-since 1993 to 1998 after an evening performance we would go to the nearest wimpy bar or favourite pub to rewind chanting poetry brains storming and discussing possible channels for our creative effort and going to sleep after hours making sure no matter how much drunk we could be we wake up on time to take a shower and a warm bath…"

If you think this is a bloody massacre of the queen's language, this is intentionally aimed at removing the blinkers that make you think there is only one way of conceptualizing reality or that the doors of linguistic and literary expression were closed once and for all with the Shakespearean and Victorian era. So, bra Ike invites you to come on and *"dash in/face reality gazilam/gova/borg/zwakala nine nine/is so maar om te se/ face daai reality? sonder oogklapies/lapha site/wasekhaya…".* The nepotism that characterizes the transition from the Apart Hate Reign of Terror to the New African Gravy Train Renounce Sense Era of Errors also comes under scrutiny in a poem entitled 'van sidlangozwane': *"van sidlangozwani/ stealing/van sidlangozwani/ skuvert under corset/ nou skiloog/ ou koeke moer se sister/ smoke down mzamo/ drum ten cook tycoon moleko/ dink jy phambili/ vole iets wonderlik or kanjani/ pump jy nou propvol/ ou koekemoer se sister/ shanty daai diesel engine/ gum gum guys bubbling gums/ wat gat aan service station…"* Knowing that Iscamtho is best experienced in a performance as the words flow like a tide, musical to their core, the publishers have made a point of providing a compact disc to accompany the book –capturing the unique voice of Ike raving: *"green caution/ yellow red read/ zaya saratoga express/ divers no victory delivery without casualty."*

FROM TONI WITH LOVE

Book: Love
ISBN: 0 7011 7510 9
Publisher: Chatto & Windus
Author: Toni Morrison

In most of her writings, from **Beloved, Jazz to Sula** and others, Toni Morrison is preoccupied with the theme of re-memorying and re-membering one's past to be able to confront the present and face the future. **Love** is vintage Toni Morrison, weaving prosaic lyrics to deliver the narratives of women battling to come to terms with a past and present, while chained to the legacy of one man, who remains at the centre of their lives, even after his death.

Cosey resort is known for its owner's knowledge of the needs of the guests as well as its hospitality, the ecstatic company of friends and the music- the cough of trumpet and piano keys waving a quarter note above the wind. As it is at any workplace, there are old alliances, mysterious battles and pathetic victories at Cosey resort. The central figure is Bill Cosey, a royal figure with an eternal laugh and embracing arms .His heart and property are the spoils his second wife, daughter-in-law, and granddaughter fight each other for. Even the waiters and the cleaners all fight for Cosy's smile. When he dies there are different opinions concerning the cause of his death. Something in Vida pushes her to believe it is a heart attack, as the doctors said. L says it is heartache, May claims it is school bussing, and Vida's husband, Saddller thinks Cosey was simply tired, "eighty one years was enough." But his enemies claim it is syphilis rampant. What Vida is certain about is that his hands reached for his stomach rather than for the chest where the heart exploded.

There is no love lost between May, the kleptomaniac daughter-in-law of Mr. Bill Cosey, her daughter Christine and Heed; the woman Cosey took for a wife at the age of eleven when his Wife Julia died. They both feel that Heed colonized the heart, the house and purse of the main man in their lives. According to May their world has been invaded and turned into a slum. Christine feels the same way, but disagrees with her mother's response. Clad in a military jacket, Che-style beret and a black leotard miniskirt, May moves from kleptomania to covering her bedroom windows with plywood painted red for danger, prophesying a violent revolution and hallucinating about being hunted down by the Black Panthers, and dies a deranged woman. Christine remains embittered by the loss of her bedroom and the attention of her grandfather, as well as her inheritance to a friend who is now supposed to be her granny.

But she returns to the house and becomes more of a servant to the woman whose quest to reclaim her husband's face and to know him and feel his love makes her resort to confining herself in a bedroom, with his photo looming above the bed. While Heed enlist the help of a half-dressed, up-country girl with gorgeous, provocative legs to write her family memoirs, Christine enlists the help of a lawyer to claim Cosey's house as hers as she's the only blood relative entitled to be called "Cosey's Girl".

But the will of the old man could not be found. Only doodles on a 1958 menu outlining his whisky-driven desires: his boat, Julia 11 to Dr Ralph, Montenegro Coronas to Chief Silk, the Hotel to Billy Boy's wife, and his '55 convertible to L. His stickpins to Meal Daddy, his record collection to Dumb Tommy, "the best blues guitar player on God's earth", and the Monarch Street house and "whatever nickels are left" to "my sweet Cosey girl". It raises everybody's eyebrows that Cosy would give Dr Ralph his newest boat. Nobody knew what Corona's he was referring to. Heed thinks Meal Daddy is the lead singer of the Purple Tones, but May says it is the manager of Fifth Street Strutters, who happens to be in prison.

Heed's claim to "my sweet Cozy child" is strengthened by the fact that she called her husband papa. But biologically speaking, Christine is the only "child" left. Only L knew who Cosy's "sweet child" was. She destroyed the original will bearing the name of Celestial, the spellbinding sporting secret woman in Cosey's life. And L is no more.

BOOK OF LOVE AND MEDITATION

Book: Avenues of My Soul
Author: Ayanda Billie
Publisher: Swii Arts Amendment
ISBN: 0-620-3485-4

Ayanda Billie started writing poetry in the mid 1980's when the demands of time and place called for poets to add their voices to those emitted by the sounding board of freedom songs. At the same time there were resonant and critical voices calling for poetry to move beyond sloganeering to an expression of personal experiences and social reality. Unlike many of today's poets who rush to a publisher with a manuscript in hand as soon as they have put ink to paper, Billie was never in haste. He patiently worked on honing his skills, approaching the craft of writing with the same amount of sensitivity and passion with which he approached his thematic material.

The result is **Avenues of my soul,** a collection of poetry that can be best described as a book of love, a scripture of meditation, a personal diary and social narrative all in one Utilizing a diverse tapestry of thematic and stylistic concerns to share the traveled and imaginary journey of the poet with readers, **"Avenues of my soul"** offers a taste of life and love in all its manifestations. It breaks the boundary between the private and public facets of life and employs narrative, in a picturesque and lyrical register, to relate the confessions of childhood crushes, erotic fantasies, reckless surrender to passion, fervent longing for childhood friends, and a passionate declaration of love for family and kin, together with the nostalgic remembrance of better days, a romantic evocation of nature and a spiritual evocation of the spirit of the ancestors along with the names of heroes (Ingoapele Madingwane, Bantu Steve Biko and Mangaliso Robert Sobukwe.)

Where local issues are addressed, the message is universal and the language has a universal appeal. The poeticization of socio-economic and political realities goes beyond sloganeering as the poet weaves the agony and pain of people into songs that stir. In the same way that social experience provides a source of inspiration, the rhythm of nature becomes a muse to the poet. But here nature is not the object of worship but a source of reflection on the power and majesty of the creator: *"Up there in the clouds/mountains of white smokes/so close to my Maker's hands/embraced by smooth waves of heavens".*

SLAM POETRY IN SOUTH AFRICA:
BEYOND THE FAD TO POETRY FOR SOCIAL CHANGE

Introduction

The 'poetry mylaitis', in particular the slam poetry bug has suddenly seized the characters in the local soapie, **"Generations"**. Kenneth Mashaba, (or is it Thomas?), brought a smile and life back into Dineo's life through the gift of a poetry book. Ntombi's crazy love for the spoken word motivated Thomas aka Mazwi to sharpen his lyrical skills in an attempt to prove that he is not merely an ardent fan of slam poetry but is a slam poet in his own right. To show they are knowledgeable on the spoken word scene in Mzansi, the **Generations'** crew even quotes the names of outstanding slam cats in Mzansi: Ntando Cele, Lexicon and Zola Sobekwa (mispronounced as Sodamu in the Soapie).

The three have appeared in the slamjam feature in Poetry Africa, which was twice won by yours truly and this year was won by Battle Rap, champ and participant at the International Slam Poetry Contest, EWOK. Apart from the Poetry Africa Slamjam, Durban has the Slam Poetry Operation Team, which runs workshops in schools, holds slam contests and also use slam poetry to address social problems like HIV/AIDS, poverty, homelessness and unemployment. In Jozi, the slam poetry scene is also picking up. At the forefront is Sound of Edutainment (SOE). Led by Prince Shapiro, SOE holds monthly Slamjams at "Horror Café" with the support of Xarra Books and T-shirt Terrorists. Among others, high-powered slam/ hip hop performers like Saul Williams, Ursula Rucker, Celena Glenn and Lemn Sissy contributed to making slam poetry a popular genre. Today the slam poetry scene is alive in many cities of the world and in South Africa/Azania there are slam poetry events even in small townships like Phuthaditjhaba in the former Bantustan of QwaQwa in eastern Free State and Zamdela Township in Sasolburg in the Vaal triangle area.

The history and origins of Slam

The emergence of slam poetry as a competitive, theatrical, participative and entertaining presentation of poetry and a social event involving a vibrant interaction between the poets and the audience is attributed to construction worker and poet, Mark Smith and the bunch of blue collar eccentric intellectuals who gathered at the Chicago jazz club, the "Get Me High Lounge" for a series of poetry sessions in 1985 and continued the tradition in the framework of the Uptown Poetry Slam at another Chicago Jazz Club, the "Green Mill" from July 25,1986 to date. Looking for a way to breathe life into the open mic poetry format, Mark Smith (Slampapi) started a poetry reading series, aided by the "Get Me High Lounge,"'s owner, the finger-popping hipster, Butchie (James Dukaris), who allowed anything to happen. The series' emphasis on performance laid the groundwork for a style of poetry and performance that would eventually be spread across the world.

In 1986 Smith approached Dave Jemilo, the owner of the "Green Mill," (a Chicago jazz club and former haunt of Al Capone) with a plan to host a weekly poetry cabaret on the club's slow Sunday nights. Jemilo welcomed him, and on July 25, the Uptown Poetry Slam was born. Smith drew on baseball and bridge terminology for the name, and instituted the show's basic structure of an open mike, guest performers, and a competition. "The Green Mill" evolved into the Mecca for performance poets, and the Uptown Poetry Slam still continues 18 years after its inception. Explaining the slam poetry craze and vibe at The Green Mill, the Idiot's Guide to declares: *"The experimenters in this new style of poetry presentation gyrated, rotated, spewed, and stepped their words along the bar top, dancing between the bottles, bellowing out the backdoor, standing on the street or on their stools, turning the west side of Chicago into a rainforest of dripping whispers or a blast furnace of fiery elongated syllables, phrases, snatches of scripts, and verse that electrified the night".*

Poetry in the Boxing ring

But in Chicago itself the idea of reading poetry in non-literary settings and in a theatrical and sporting and somewhat eccentric and experimental style often bordering on a break with conventions, could be traced back to as early as the late1970s and early 1980s. Sometime in 1978 (or 1979) Jerome Salla and Elaine Equi gave readings at Facets Multimedia. Elaine Equi recalls, *"Jerome was getting bigger audiences, drawing from bars, the Art Institute scene, from clubs such as"* O'Banyon's,"" La Mer", *artists, and publishers. The people around the "Body Politic" were one scene. But when Jerome and I would read, it was not really a literary competition crowd"* By 1980 Salla constructed his own poetry based on a boxing match and the crowd was rowdy. Elaine Equi explains how this started: *"My husband was reading at some space in Chicago... His readings were always accompanied by a lot of audience participation. There was one particular musician, named Jimmy Desmond, who got irritated easily when he was drunk. He grabbed a chair and swung at Jerome. There was a fight, but it didn't actually come to blows."* Jerome Salla continues, *"A couple days later I got call from Al-Simmons. He was involved with the old poetry scene in New York's lower east side, and in Chicago too, and hung with Ted Berrigan. He said, 'Jimmy Desmond would like to challenge you to a ten-round poetry fight to the death.'."* (Kurt Heintz, 1996)

Pioneer of the slam poetry scene in New York, Bob Holman recalls seeing Ted Berrigan and Ann Waldman in a poetry bout dressed in boxing gear around 1979, but indicates that he didn't first communicate with Mark Smith until after he visited the "Green Mill" in person. Elaine Equi proposes that Simmons might have got the idea from , from professional wrestling, but also adds that Simmons told her that he saw a couple of poets in a boxing ring in New York and would love to stage a poetry fight between her and Simmons.

The first fight took place in 1980 at a fly-by-night club. Equi has very fresh memories of these 'poetry fights': *"I read a poem called 'Give Piss a Chance' shortly after the death of John Lennon, and the crowd booed.. They had a stage like a boxing ring and girls in bikinis, holding up cards for the number of the rounds. They also had and judges... each round Jerome and Jimmy reading one poem. Jerome won. It was not a fluke. They had a rematch and he won again. About two hundred people witnessed the second match. Their match was at "Tut's" on Belmont at Sheffield, now "The Avalon". I read in leather boxing shorts, had a robe that said Baby Jerome. Jimmy had a nickname too. We didn't really hate each other. It was just a funny, kind of weird event we threw to make money,"* says Salla. *"There was little story in the Trib. We were with the punk scene. A lot of forces were converging in Chicago at the same time. Suddenly there was an audience for poetry. There really isn't anything that close to the experience today except in rap music."* (Kurt Heintz, 1996)

The philosophies of slam

Equi's reference to rap in relation to the late 1970's poetry phenomenon in Chicago is interesting given the link that today's slam poetry has with hip hop, of which rap is one of the components. It is noteworthy that Mark Smith took the name from the game of basketball, which has also had a cordial relationship with hip hop. Based on this information, one can say with slam poetry, Mark Smith and his crew of convention-busting poets and lovers of the spoken word continued a tradition that -in Chicago-started in the late 70's, and gave it a format and name in tune with the times. Perhaps confirming the communality spirit of Slam and the universal nature of its ideal of creating an open space for expression, Mark Smith declares on his website that Slam does not belong to him but to "the thousands of people who have dedicated their time, money, and energy to this Chicago-born, interactive format for presenting poetry to a public that has a zillion other barks and belches and flashes to hold its attention. However he expresses his wish that the Slam phenomenon will grow in accordance with the philosophies that have become what he considers the backbone of what we call the "Slam Family":

- The purpose of poetry (and indeed all art) is not to glorify the poet but rather to celebrate the community to which the poet belongs. (This idea is paraphrased from the works of Wendell Berry)
- The show and the show's effect upon the audience are more important than any one individual's contribution to it.
- The points are not the point; the point is poetry. (Alan Wolfe)
- The performance of poetry is an art -- just as much an art as the art of writing it.
- NO audience should be thought of as obligated to listen to the poet. It is the poet's obligation to communicate effectively, artfully, honestly, and professionally so as to compel the audience to listen.
- The slam should be open to all people and all forms of poetry.
- With respect to its own affairs, each slam should be free from attachment to any outside organization and responsible to no authority other than its own community of poets and audience.
- NO group, individual, or outside organization should be allowed to exploit the Slam Family.
- We must all remember that we are each tied in some way to someone else's efforts. Our individual achievements are only extensions of some previous accomplishment.
- Success for one should translate into success for all.
- The National Slam began as a gift from one city to another. It should remain a gift passed on freely to all newcomers.
(http://www.slampapi.com/new_site/background/philosophies.htm)

Towards an organic South African Slam Movement

These are lofty communalistic and humanistic ideas that in the dog-eat-dog individualistic and materialistic society might be easily dismissed as far too idealistic and utopian. Mark Smith himself confesses that "the idealism and cooperative forces of the slam are in constant conflict with the competitive and self-serving appetites of its ambitious nature". He asserts that the struggle between the idealism of slam and its competitive spirit has taught the Slam family much but also threatens to obliterate all that it has grown to be. Unequivocally and unambiguously he declares that he is "on the side of idealism and hope".

How many of us who have latched onto the slam poetry buzz share this idealism and pro-humanism spirit? And to what extent are we able to contextualise the slam movement to the tangible and concrete realities of Azania and locate it within the particularities and peculiarities of the Azanian/South African situation? How do we relate the slam movement to our own history of using poetry in particular and literature and theatre in general to open the space of discourse and critical engagement with the prevailing socio-economic, political and cultural conditions? Can we draw from the experiences of pre-colonial African oral traditions to develop an organically grown and contextualised slam poetry movement in South Africa/Azania?

In South Africa/Azania the idea of doing poetry in a non-literary setting and of moving out of Euro-centric conventions with regard to the stylistic concerns of poetry and the manner in which it is delivered, is not a new phenomena. As early as the 1970's, groups like Dashiki fused poetry with jazz. The Allah Poets, Mihloti, Medupi Writers and others recited their poetry over the beat of a drum and sounds of horns. People like Muthobi Motloatse and Gamakhulu Diniso of Busang Thakaneng used the term Proemdra to refer to a fusion of prose, poetry, music and drama, and promoted the notion of participatory theatre. Muthobi Motloatse's theatre piece, **'Nkosi - the Healing song'** is a typical example of the fusion of the language of story telling, music, dance and drama. Here the barriers between the audience and the performer were broken down, and in the words of a character in **'Nkosi - the Healing Song'**, "myths, legends and facts are interwoven and the story can 'begin in the ending and end in the middle' ".

The concept of participatory theatre that gained ground in the 70's and 80's was informed not only by 'the anti-poetry theory' of Bertold Brecht, Jerry Grotowsky's 'poor theatre' and Augusto Boal's "theatre of the oppressed," but also by pre-colonial African Cultural and artistic forms of expression, where there were no rigid borderlines between music, poetry, dance, etc. When groups like Ujamaa (in Sharpeville), Rakgalema Medupi Arts Commune and Arts in Motion (in Sebokeng), Mafube (in the East rand) and Makana Poets (in Zamdela) emerged in the 1980's and 1990's, they followed the same trend began by their predecessors.

These groups performed poetry at political rallies and social events like wedding ceremonies and birthday parties, at schools, in churches, in beer-halls and in stadiums. Poetry was in prisons, in hostels, in squatter camps and in refugee camps, and in the trenches and guerrilla training camps in exile. In the words of Muthobi Motlaotse, this kind of literature and theatre deliberately shit on conventional English-English literary forms. It mixed languages and genres and knew no holy cows. In as far as its dare-devil, passionate and energetic, genre-crossing, convention-defying and multi-media spirit and its effort to open up space for self-expression and dialogue between the writer and society is concerned, the slam poetry phenomenon, shares stylistic and thematic concerns with the poetry, literary and theatre movement of the 1970's up to the early 90's in South Africa/Azania. The efforts of many slam poets/hip hop activists in Azania today to attune their artistic expressions to the historical-material experiences, politico-economic conditions and the cultural and linguistic heritage of Azania/South Africa, is in many ways a continuation of the tradition and legacy of the 1970's generation that was in the main inspired by the philosophy of Black Consciousness.

Conclusion

What is missing is a conscious and well coordinated programme to link up the present literary and cultural movement with the past and to educate the current crop of poets and cultural activists about their predecessors. The ignorance of the present-day generation of poets and spoken word activists about the contributions and achievements of their predecessors and ancestors in the literary world is reflected by the little respect shown to the legendary Mafia Pascal Gala during his recital at Poetry Africa. The impatient audience heckled Gala when he recited at the opening day of Poetry Africa. The presenter of the programme is to blame for not informing the audience that Gwala was entitled to recite for more than the four minutes allocated to other poets, as he was the featured poet of the day. He also introduced Gwala with one sentence whereas he went on and on about the other poets.

Given a proper direction, the poetry movement and the cultural movement in South Africa have a lot to offer to this country. And acknowledging the struggles, contributions and efforts of our predecessors in the South African literary and theatre movement and learning from them would be the first step in the right direction. Names that come to mind are Mirriam Tladi, Fatima Dike, Fikile Magadlela, Nardine Gordimer; Richard Rive, James Mathews, Strini Moodley (who founded the first union of Black theatre and at whose request Gwala wrote the classical piece, 'The Children of Nonti'), Mafika Gwala, Mazisi Kunene, Farouk Asvat, Benjy Francis, Athol Fugard, John Kani, Lefifi Tladi, Lesego Rampolokeng. The list is endless. The passion of most of these individuals for literature and theatre was fanned by the desire to use the word as an instrument for transformation and social change. Their works were part of the quest for a South Africa and a world with a more human face. It is this understanding that will motivate the present-day writer, poet and artist to use podiums like the slam poetry/spoken word scene as mediums of self-expression, as well as a platform for social dialogue and an instrument for social change. When this happens the word will not cower before the dictates of capital but will place the collective dignity and collective interests and aspirations of the people before narrow materialistic individual gains.

Sources

1.   www.slampapi.com/new-site/background.htm (accessed on 10\11\06)
2.   http://www.slampapi.com/new_site/background/philosophies.htm(accesses on 13\11\06)
3.   http://www.e-poets.net/library/slam/converge.html (accessed on 13\11\06)

Thina lomhlaba siugezile: The Poetic Voice of a South Africa in Transition

Introduction

Social reality is the womb within which art and literature is born, as well as the object mirrored in art and literature, but it is also the reality from which art and literature often flee so as to portray the world neither as it is or ought to be but as it exists in the dreams, visions and imaginations of the artist and the writer. Literary works have historic specificity in that they capture the spirit of a time and place and are born at particular times and in a specific place, but they are not necessarily bound by time and place in that they sometimes deliberately set out to demolish the boundaries of time and space. South African, particularly Black Writings in the times of the struggle had the expository and commentary function of exposing and critiquing the system, presenting a visionary challenge in their futuristic role of pointing out the path to the future and envisaging a South Africa free from racial-capitalism...an Azania of the free and the bold. Novels such as Mongane Wally Serote's **To Every Birth its Blood** and Miriam Tladi's **Amandla** did not stop at a journalistic exposition of the evils of Apartheid capitalism and an epic portrayal of the people's struggle. They offered the reader a vision of the envisaged emancipated Azania.

This dual function of commenting on the present and painting a vision of the future comes out very clear in Mothubi Motloatse's **Ngwana Wa Azania.** The piece is futuristic in its thematic as well as stylistic concerns. It predicts a future where the child of zwepe and madice will achieve liberation with TNT and restore the long forgotten isintu, Mangwana o thswara thipa ka bohaleng, and at the same time paves the way towards a post-Euro-centric writing in Azania. This is the kind of literature written about Apartheid South Africa, which transcends the South African mindset to write and dream an equalitarian Azania. Ingoapele Madigwane articulated the cry for Africa's tormented soul in **Africa, My Beginning** *(They laid down their sponges/ flat on its soil/ to absorb its resources)*, but painted a picture and vision of unity and freedom *(In the heart of Africa/ Africans shall meet as one/ And Africa utaswema kiswahil to seal the African bond/ how I wish to be in that part of Africa/ And drink from the calabash/ umuthi we nkululeko)*, ultimate victory and reconstruction *(Renaissance. The time for the rediscovery of Africa by African's has now dawned.)*

As the process of transition began in South Africa some critics argued that South African Writers would face a crisis because their main source of reference and inspiration was *The Black Experience* under Apartheid capitalism. This neocolonial argument ignored the fact that Post-Apartheid South Africa, with its inherently neocolonial, neocapitalist character would itself continue to make *The Black Experience* and the conditions of the working and underclasses of the land, a viable source of reference and inspiration for South African Writers in the same way that it has been and still is for African Writers in the rest of post-independence, neocolonial Africa. For as long as neocolonial South Africa would continue to be a country where poor people died from poverty and squalor while the rich and propertied people died from eating too much- and the poor happened to be predominately Black - *the Black Experience* would, dialectically and logically, be the point of departure for the initiatives of writers to write about the transition from Apartheid capitalism to neocolonial capitalism and point the way to de-colonialization. Indeed writers would always seize a moment like this to search for alternative routes that took them beyond the current reality to new terrains where no one has trod before. This would be reflected in both the thematic as well as technical aspects of the literary works.

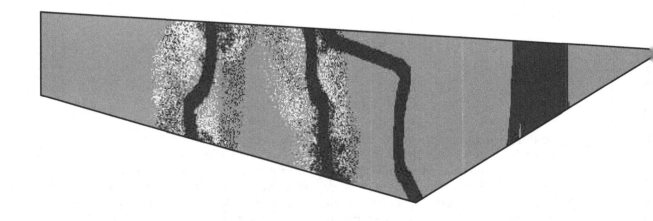

In search of New Voices

In checking out the direction South poetry is taking we will analyse the poems published in **Botstotso Magazine,** a literary journal which gives a podium to new and emerging writers whose writings capture the spirit of the time and place, namely 21st century, post-Apartheid South Africa, and also provide reflections of the past and a re-construction and de-construction of the South African Story. We will also take a microscopic look at the poetry appearing in **The Virtual Anthology,** a web page initiated by Mike Cope with the intention of collecting the core of what may later become *a larger representation of contemporary South African Poetry (Cope: 2000).* Why choose these two publications? Cope issued the call for submission of poems in 2000 and restricted the submission period to one year, with the deadline date being April 16, 2001. For the most part, the poets who responded sent poems which were not published anywhere before. Understanding that they were submitting their works for an anthology, the poets naturally handpicked and submitted the poems they considered their best. There is a fair balance in terms of the gender and the race of the poets in **The Virtual Anthology** and a great deal of diversity in terms of the stylistic, technical aspects and thematic concerns of the poems. **Botsotso magazine** is particularly relevant because of the concept of collaborative composition and collective editing as popularized by the then Botsotso Jesters in the Botsotso Magazine and anthologies such as **WE JIVE LIKE THIS, DIRTY WASHING** and **NO FREE SLEEPING,** the idea of fusing poetic forms of artistic expression and the visual arts and (of late) the concept of acousto-electronic poetry, which developed out of experimentation between the **Botsotso Poets** and James De Villiers of 111 Studio and resulted in the poetry CD, **PURPLE LIGHT MIRROR IN THE MUD.**

Another interesting point about the **Botsotso Poets** is that it constitutes a multiplicity of poetic voices in terms of both the technical and thematic aspects of the works…from the muso-poetic Allan Kolski Horwitz, the dub-influenced social critique rapper, Siphiwe Ka Ngwenya, to the light-hearted streetwise, jazzy Iscamtho poetry of Ike Mboneni Muila, evocative of the Sophiatown Renaissance, and from the high-fluting imagery- loaded lyrics of Isabella Motadinyane deeply ingrained in the commentary "call a spade a spade"' traditions of the Basotho, to the tight , complicated rhyme-schemed verse of Lionel Murcott and the raw, punk/poetic surrealism of Clinton Du Plessis who writes mostly in Afrikaans.

Iscamtho Poetry or Kwaito Poetry

Botsotso publishes works in all South African languages including township slang often erroneously referred to as Tsotsi Taal, but known to its speakers and the poets who use it as Iscamtho. The magazine and the Botsotso Jesters, now known as the Botsotso Poets, share the defiant, avant-garde, hip and adventurous spirit of exploration and self-expression with their namesake, the tight, bum-revealing jean which symbolizes the non-conformist, carefree spirit of the hip, punk sub-culture which manifests itself in the form of the different trends which seize the youth in different eras, and vary from country to country, but was sizzled in the furnace of resistance in South Africa:

One leg in
another leg out
tight me up
strongly sewn
visible mending
back pocket trademark
silver buttons attached
not woven once
twice or thrice
Die' is mos botsotsos
back pocket
front pocket
mog n' mal talk to me
pull high
stretch on a high way
ons pedestry met doves
no attention no whistler no weebit
no hearing sweet nothings
strongly sewn
Die' is mos botsotsos.

Motadinyane in "One Leg In" from **Purple Light Mirror In The Light**

Iscamtho poetry mainly articulates the ethos and vibes of the Sophia Town/Kofifi Renaissance and the flamboyant, but rebellious, anti-system and anti-uppity sepantsula sub-culture:

Grasshopper dash silver bended soul finger
Sportless munich machine
Ignite pre-mature
Undefined cabin cruiser under the sun
On a dirty washing day
Memories flock against
The direction of the wind
Jitterbug kofifi dance
Turkey shoe unmarked
Two tone mooi mark
Backbone spinner
Thina lomhlaba siugezile
Nge mellow yellow maize
Mielie meal stranded
Green line troja strictly prohibited
Spectacle goggle smoking eyes off
Beer bottle tobacco and drug sniffing cocaine
For healthy reasons rizzla belt
Phuza face rash
Straight and two beers
Mail boxer jive
Iwisa eating crust
From the pot spectacular
Chaff kop makoko grap
Half barren maize mielie meal pizza
Freeze a lot of eat and drink available
Children playing in the playground
No dumping space here
Three quarter wear
Induna spectator
First gear beshu
Change down second hand
Mellow yellow
Maize mielie meal
Bag tea shirt.

Ike Mboneni Muila in **"Worn Out Dirty Washing"** from **Purple Light Mirror In The Mud**

Making full use of poetic license Iiscamtho poetry skilfully fuses languages to give the reader/viewer a full view of the South African Landscape and mindscape in a pictorial, humorous language, which particularly captures the noises and nuances of township South Africa. Its social commentary moves from the trivial to the serious and from to the serious to the mundane with ease in the same way that it masks a serious voice of political analysis and cultural struggle behind "simple talk":

> Ke sukasihambe
> Msakazo we sizulu
> Basopa platform one
> Kusuka amaphepha
> Kusala amac-cardbox
> Isikhathi siyashwabana Wasekhaya
> Mampara kite
> Mochochonono crazy
> Jigsaw puzzle
> Squealer ry plus one
> Minus one problem
> Vole hebe hebe
> Moshumo haba haba
> Oxin tailor kgashu
> Ek slat hulle nou die laaste
> School bar no drakes
> Tot elke voeel
> In sy nis is
> Of kanjani
> Of hoe se^ ek
> Nou die laaste
> Madala side caution
> Welele ebukhosini
> Sharp over bakhiwa
> Hola…
> Mochochonono crazy
> Jigsaw puzzle
> Kite Milky Way
> Ha bonolo feela..
> Dance Milky Way
> Snakes ladder
> Banana ka bhasela
> Donsa
> Ba rekisa malana le mohodu
> Madombolo le magwinya
> Wrong site surveyor
> Mdakeni
> Stick in the mud

Ike Mboneni Muila in Mochochonono Crazy from **Purple Light Mirror In The Mud**

It easily articulates the serious through a playful-like, silly-witty lingo, and gives you the rare opportunity to see South Africa and the Black township Experience through the eyes of the carefree danger-chasing Tsotsi, the ever-jovial comedian, the independent-minded freethinker and the carefree, the journalistic gossiper and vulgar taxi-driver:

Touting, touting taxi
Topsy turvy
Pep talk
From Zola to jozi
Music background
Loud and loud
Pep talk
Trace toilet tissue
Tracks
Bo ke bona dibono
Ke sa bone beng ba tsona
Taxi topsy-turvy
Pep talk
Constant thuggery
Criss cross
Cross-pollination
Christianity charged
Short cut corner
Magomsha style
Corner market and nugget
Taxi topsy-turvy pep talk
Drinking beefeaters eyes off
Melting bazookas
Meaty juice
Ba harela jwala eka ba kgaohile maoto
Kwala molomo lovey
Ke mametse
Touting taxi topsy-turvy
Pep talk.

Isabella Motadinyane in **"Touting Taxi"** from **Purple Light Mirror In The Mud**

Behind the humor lies a philosophic reflection on the joys and sorrows of being South African, the light and darker side of township reality. Tapping into his extraordinary gift of crafting as many as five languages in one poem, Mboneni specifically treats the reader to the melodious tapestry of Tshivenda, one of the most marginalized, minority languages of South Africa:

Kha ndi sekene mutshini yani
Kha u lile ludzula back door
Ndi madhuva mana
La vhutanu ndi mutshinyalo
Vhusiku sala nduni
Ha madala khakhu nga life.

Ike Mboneni Muila in **"Madice"** from **Purple Light Mirror In The Mud**

Venda ni si luvhe nga mufhetano
Mbuyavhuhadzi yo vhulela
Zwi la zwa madekewe
Vho munyalo khotsi salani
King corn manzhanzha mthmbo
Mmela ni vha lumelise.

The aesthetic influences of Iscamtho/ Kwaitoetry and contemporary Black Poetry in general ranges from the oral traditions to Dub-poetry and Jazzoetry in the mould of The Last Poets Mutabaruka, Linton Kwesi Johnson, Jane Cortez, popular music, particularly jazz to nursery rhymes and traditional and contemporary township children's games:

Piki piki mabalane
sala sala gentleman
nda wana vhana
vha tshi khou tamba
vha
tshi
imbelela
tshinoni
vha tshiri thungununu
nemulambo
nemulambo kumedza. . .
piki piki mabalane
sala sala gentleman
over billy bok
akaka billy bok
inch inch inch
as one as two
aga jeremia sies-tog
puma wena sala wena
piki piki mabalane
sala sala gentleman
hoor net dae blend
two skyf saggies
madakeni
stick in the mud
bova cathawane
sixteen. . .

A translation from Venda:

i found children playing
singing for the bird
singing river bird
singing river bird
river bird catch a nap. . .

(Muila: 2000)

Iscamtho poetry is in itself a deliberate act of sabotage. It consciously challenges Euro-centric literary conventions and purposefully contaminate *suiwer* Afrikaans and English-English with *Sjita-Scamtho* so as to combat their domination of the linguistic and literary scene as well as the academic terrain and ideological discourse:

Hulle omitted onse lingo
Innie list van official languages
So dat ons moet met ndlondlo kies
Tussen speak en praat
Ons het body language graag gekies
Hulle het gedink dis maar empty talk
Maar kapzella het tension gerelease
En high blood pressure gereduce
Monkey jive het shit-parade development gelag
Thula mabota het artificial barriers gebreek
Codesa jive announced die einde
Van apart hate era of terror
En die begin van African Gravy Train Renounce sense
Era of errors
Hulle gesels nie meer
Die cell phone doen die werk
Hulle praat nie meer
Die voice mail soelat overtime
Scamtho's alive and kicking.

(Bofelo 2001: 96)

Iscamtho and hip pop lingo has even infiltrated journalism, resulting in a witty, rap-laced, lyrical journalistic genre such as the one in the pieces by Vusi Khumalo in Pace Magazine and Kgafela Oa Magogodi in YMag:

"Dis page shall speak of poets who like to lick the mic...of poets igniting the word lamps of our times with their rhymes and free verse. **Dis page pays tribute to the poetic genius of all the verse mongers who gave voice to waves of performance poetry in the land of the fallen rand.** Dis page is a celebration of spoken word poetry and its makers in Mzansi and beyond. **Dis page shall be called THE WORD."**

(Magogodi: 2002)

 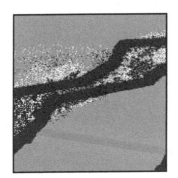 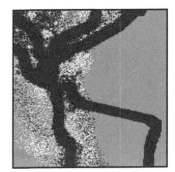

Tackling diverse issues with a multiplicity of poetic techniques

Varying between lyrics, carefully rhyme-schemed poetry, free verse and prose-poetry in terms of style and technique, South African poetry in general tackles a variety of subjects and encapsulates a variety and diversity of voices from the neoromantic escape into nature from society, a neomodernist critique of the existing order, a postmodernist celebration of diversity, a postcolonial articulation of the center-margin discourse to a pro-decolonialization and Marxian castigation of globalization and a critique of the neocolonial set-up in South Africa. It is not unusual for one poet to move from one theme to another and from one style to the other, depending on the theme s/he is tackling and the atmosphere s/he wishes to create, the mood s/he wants to express and the tone/tune in which s/he chose to speak/sing. Moving from the public sphere to the private realm of existence, from national politics to bedroom politics or the politics of the center as they are called in the jargon of Uniqwa Students, Isabella Motadinyane extols the chemistry/charm of the female body and the beauty and the joy of making love:

Dark night babe
Toss and turn
The clouds above
You make the sober go drunk
Come in from the cold
Warm you up
Sink down our throat
The clouds above
Mountain so high
Sink babe sink
Sink a shaft
Move slowly down the mountain
Down our throats
Toss and turn babe
Sink on me
All night
In dark clouds above
You make the sober go drunk
Sink babe sink
Sink it smooth
Sink a shaft.

Anna Varney joins in the poetic extolling and exaltation
of the joyous experience of lovemaking:

Pulsing sweaty sweet
Hands moulds my moves
Last night-
How we danced!
Butterfly kisses
Hot muscle
Throb
Liquidsliding
I want to lie with you.

At same she looks inside herself and finds an emptiness:

Empty
Through what eyes
What vision
Do I project?
When I look inside

I speak
Now hesitating
Now clear
From where come the words
When I look inside
Empty

Like music
Unchanging
Feelings but not emotion
Like love truly
What is joy?
What is sorrow?
I am an inheritance
A culmination
An interpretation
When I look inside
I see no future.

She is also capable of empathizing with the poor downtrodden,
unemployed, perhaps homeless and shackless working class woman
who drowns her sorrows in a bottle of beer, or maybe metholated spirits:

She had nothing
So she drank
All her money
She has nothing
So she drinks
She is lost
But first
She lost everything
Then she drank
Now she drinks
She can't get work
That's why she's drunk
She won't get work
She drinks
She drinks
Because why
She's drunk.

Anna Varney goes further to voice out the radical, anarchist cry for the complete obliteration of all structures so as to free the individual from the beast of state and the claws of social control:

Ban the political parties
Ban the organizations
Ban the temples
All structures must be banned

What about the home
The work places

What about the ice-cream cart?

Something may come of it
The day is very gray
Cold
Outside a bell tinkles
A lone man
Pushes his dreams.

Anna Varney in **"Unity"** from **Purple Light Mirror in the Mud**

The contradiction between the inner peace found from genuine love, human relationship and nature's beauty and the alienating impact of the forces of social control is perhaps captured more eloquently in the poetry of Rustum Kozain. He laments the fact that neither night nor dawn brings comfort to wretched souls, cries against the rape of the people of the South by the IMF and other institutions of global capitalism and the ravage of modernism on love. He further decrys the impoverishment of the poor by low salaries and high taxes and the national budget which is unfriendly to the poor in the land of the condom and a hypocritical world of empty slogans, unimplemented charters and accords, false handshakes and obscene soap operas in the mist of chattering guns, and lambastes the neo-colonial state of affairs where *the radicals drive and are driven in limozines and host dinners to court capital, promising restitution, flashing a smile in shark-skin suits,* as we become more and more a people of squatters, *building zink and cardboard hopes over the words that scratch at our reformed lives.*

He, however, finds solace and hope in the flower slashing through the hoped for night out, the bass guitar of Linton Kwesi Johnson strumming a liberating rhyme, the open sky, and he soldiers on because of the love of a hometown that has kept him close to earth and close to the people he has grown to love.

Maintaining the balance between private and public life

Being the soul of the nation, poetry has at all times been locked in the struggle to strike the balance between the rights and responsibilities of the individual towards society and the rights and responsibilities of society towards the individual as well as the balance between the rights and needs of humankind to explore and extract from nature for survival and sustenance and the need to preserve and protect the earth, the air and the ozone layer from human folly and the destructive impulse of human beings. Poetry also faces the challenge of striking the balance between freeing the voice of the individual from the Bigger Noise of Social Control and combating the anarchic tendency to take poetry as a passport away from social reality and to use poetic license as an excuse to be insensitive to the collective dreams, visions and aspirations, fears and hopes of society and the common good of humankind.

South African Poetry in English was born within the womb of settler-colonialism and an educational, social, economic, cultural and political environment in which there was and there continue to be a clash between the dominant discourse on the arts propounding the notion of art for its own sake or literature as an end in itself, and poetry as nothing more than a craft and the alternative position advocating arts with a social function, an awareness-raising literature and a poetry which is a medium of conscientization and spreader of the gospel of change and transformation. In South Africa there has always been a debate whether, while playing their role as the legislators of society and its watchdogs, the poets and artists in general should also avoid being part of the propaganda machinery of the party, the state, the church and so on, and so forth. The major challenge faced by poets has always been fulfilling the desire to protect the individual voice from being swallowed by the voice of the crowd, while at the same time fulfilling the desire to express the voice of the people. South African poetry also faced the challenge of grappling with the present, while at the same time re-constructing the past and confronting the future.

The major challenge of post-Apartheid poetry was therefore, to capture the spirit of transition from Apartheid/settler colonialism and racial-capitalism, to offer an in-depth analysis and critique of a post-Apartheid, neocolonial, neocapitalist South Africa and provide a vision of hope for the future. De-colonialzation means an anti-racist society in which every citizen is treated as an individual and the state does not encroach on the right of the individual to be and to belong. The more and more the poet tries to comprehend the past, the more and more s/he is forced to look back, and the more and more s/he confronts the future, the more and more the past haunts him/her.

This experience becomes more complicated and at times very painful in a country like South Africa, where the past includes the rape and plunder and erosion of the land, the marginalisation of the culture and the denial of the humanity and dignity of one group by another on the basis of colour and the artificial division of race, and where the future most certainly depends heavily on the extent to which reconciliation and restoration in the form of reparation and re-distribution of the land and its wealth and resources as well as the re-humanization of the historically dispossessed, de-humanised and brutalized through a moral regeneration initiative as well as atonement on the part of the former colonizers. For the formerly colonized, it is a matter of learning to forgive without having to forget. The situation and tragedy of the former colonizers is graphically captured and beautifully articulated by the persona in Gillian Schutte's poem, **"Chasing the Ancestors"**. Scorched from the warm embrace of the land she thought belonged only to her, asking herself why and when that message was encoded in her DNA She feels/sees:

Ghosts stirring nastily in their
Sanguine comfort zones
Hear the shattering of dreams
Crushed between the
Disparity of our histories
The primordial scream
Which is yet to be heard
And I know I came here
Chasing your ancestors
But instead
I danced the waltz of death with mine.

Schutte.2001:68

The poems reviewed thus far, reflect divergent ways through which South African poets have attempted to fulfil the function of re-reading the past, objectively and well as subjectively, scrutinizing the present and portraying their own visions of tomorrow. They reflect an interfusing of the dreams and nightmares, fears and hopes, visions and aspirations of the individual with the collective experiences, nightmares and dreams, hopes and fears, aspirations and visions of the society/nation/ in the world where the globe is turned into an American village. Indeed South African poetry will at all times grapple with and express the yearning for a sense of time and place, and continue to struggle against the colonialzation of public life by politicians - or as Jeremy Cronin puts it, the men in grey suits - and endeavour to liberate private life from colonialzation by **The Bold and The Beautiful, Days of Our Lives, Generations** and **Isidingo.**

As an embodiment of and an integral part of South African culture which faces the threat of being eroded by the McDonald and Coca-Cola culture, South African poetry cannot but cry against the turning of the globe into an American Village and the moral decadence that results from all the cultural suffocation emanating from the Americanization of South Africa:

> *"Die Americans is in die strate*
> *Die digters is rokkende rappers*
> *Die prieste is paniekbevange pedofiele*
> *Die jong seuns dra oorbele*
> *Die meisies dra swangaer aan lewe …..*
> *Die skrywers is beroemd in buiteland*
> *Die prekers word oordonder deur tupac shakur*
> *& puff daddy*
> *die maagde dra mandrax in hulle lope*
> *die lyke blom rosrooi onder wit lakens*
> *op die sypaadjies*
> *die 26 is in die strate*
> *die seuns dra caterpillars*
> *die clever kids stamp en stoot nog clever kids die lewe in*
> *die meisies dra designer jeans*
> *die bende is bevry*
> *Daar is geen kinders in die strate."*

Du Plesis 2001:13

CONLUSION

Simply put, South African Poetry, particularly the poetry by Black South Africans, has not ceased from being the poetry of resistance, awareness/consciousness - raising and conscientisation. It continues to be the voice of the voiceless and silent majority in the new struggles - the struggle against super-exploitation of labour by global capital, the struggle against poverty and HIV/AIDS and the struggle against the culture of looting and corruption by the kleptomaniac oligarchy... the struggle for land, the struggle for reparation and the restoration of the pride and dignity of the marginalized and socially disenfranchised majority. It shall continue to sing the joy of the exotically beautiful landscapes as well as the song of a people who take out the frustrations of waiting in vain for the ferry to the Promised Land that never comes.

References
1.   Kolski Horwitz, A (ed) **5 Poetry** 2001. Botsotso Publishing: Joubert Park
2.   **Purple Light Mirror in the Mud.** Botsotso\111Productions
3.   **Virtual Anthology:** http\\www.cope.co.za.Virtual.content\htm
4.   **Y Mag.** April 2002 NUMBER 38.

AGAINST THE TYRANNY OF TIME AND PLACE

Review of Poetic License by Mike Alfred (Botsotso Publishing, 2007)

The poetry of Mike Alfred situates itself in time and place (21st century Johannesburg) and yet launches outside the limits of time and place in its interrogation of the pressures exerted on Johannesburg and the facelift imposed on her physique and psyche by the histrionics and mechanics of socio-political changes, the hand of industry and the forces of the market. Whether it is an articulation of personal history with or within a specific place (as in **Yeoville**), or a social and psychological commentary-through individual perspectives of characters on the margin/periphery of Joburg city - (as in **I saw a man**), the personal and social concerns and issues that are raised in the course of this critical examination of the various corners, places and spaces of Johannesburg are universal. The love-hate relationship that is reflected in the frank conversations with industrial, inner-city and suburban Johannesburg is typical of most relationships between the individual and his/her city (or between citizen and country). A city often betrays one's dreams and aspirations for a more clean, safe and healthy environment, as well as a more peaceful and secure world, yet it still remains his/her one and only beloved home.

Indeed Jozi is both home and muse to Mike Alfred; so much so that it becomes the avenue and metaphor through which he reaches out to the world, connecting with every person in the world, who has fears and hopes and dreams and nightmares about the time and place s/he lives in, and who is always reflecting on his/her relationship to the house (and home and family), street, city, suburb (or ghetto), that s/he finds himself in. Reflections on places and the poet's past and present place in these places spark recollections of haunting moments and memories that rudely awaken him to the reality that the past is not always rosy but contains haunting and painful experiences:
"Where, listening through a closed door to/ raised voices, I learnt about my father's womanizing."

An examination of places, buildings and spaces in Johannesburg serves to expose the ravages of the worship of capital accumulation, the deity of economic growth and the cult of consumerism on natural and social surroundings, particularly the devastation of the landscape of Johannesburg and the psyche of her people - who are in essence her limb and body, heart and soul. A clear example of this is the opening poem in the collection; **34 Collingwood St,** which is a lamentation over the harmful intrusion of man and the machine into nature. It begins with a nostalgic reminiscence of the time when *"the stream was not a gutter/ when water dribbled from moss between stones"* expresses a longing for the tranquility and peace of the time *"when the antelope drank at dusk and lions coughed on/ white swept mornings"* and decries environmental degradation and social decay:
"once, no iron roofs, ringing in the sun/ no bar brawls or little litter, no exotic forest with Lorries and Barbers."

Yet in the midst of the turbulence and destruction the poet finds solace in the resilience, endurance, timelessness and invincibility of the natural and cosmic world: *"The same wind blows, carrying the scent of the elephant/ which we do not recognize/ Mists erase the city/ Thunder, hail and lightening thrash the slopes/ The sky we know surrounds the world, and lizards lounge forever."*

However Mike Alfred's poetic critique of the devastations of the market on Johannesburg is not in the manner of a romantic and obscurantist escape into nature or some pre-lapsarian idyllic past. In **At a Party** he exposes the hypocrisy of the elites who spend thousands of rands to go fishing in Alaska and romanticize the African landscape but are paranoid of its people: *"An Irish brogue? told me about his fulfilled life, marred only/ by his residential proximity to Soweto."*

In **Ah Joburg** he speaks in/through the voice of subaltern people who rush to Johannesburg in search of the dream of a better life, only to receive the short end of the capitalist stick. This is a cry of rage against the rich who make money on the backs of the poor and at the expense of polluting the air the poor breathe daily, but confine the poor to squalor while they hide behind the safety and security of electric fences and boom-gates:

> *"You golden skinflint capitalist bastion*
> *You hide behind fences and turncoats with guns*
> *You herd us into the seedier parts of town*
> *You curse the cardboard shanties over our heads*
> *You sell us clapped smoking cars*
> *You mouth great psalm of black empowerment*
> *We're sick and tired of Patrick Motsepe TV*
> *You close your eyes and prattle about collateral*
> *You chase our traders off the streets*
> *You provide no transport."*

There is also a frustrating feeling of entrapment to the city and to the life of selling labor and soul to capital: *"And still we smile and/ beg to mow your lawns/ beg to clean your toilets/ while you look past us."* But beneath there is a raging subversive and rebellious voice of utter disgust at the status quo that subjects people to the life of mere survival instead of living:

"Oh yes we saunter in front of your BMWs / Piss in your parks and strew them with rubbish / Yes when we are not aching with smile we stare at you / We dice and weave and hoot you when the lights turn yellow/ And we taunt your policemen and turn your officials into collaborators/ And we beg and steal and sell drugs and prostitute ourselves/ Forgive us please for raising capital and gleaning influence/ Do you teach only survival/ Good man, smiling widely / As we guard your cars".

The survivalist spirit is not in the sense of pessimistic resignation to the state of affairs, as the voice of the poor place demands of the establishment: *"Show us a job/ better show us a career/ something to make life meaningful"*, and chastises Joburg and the system for offering no alternative ways out of the doldrums: *"you focus our minds so sharply/ you're one merciless bastard of a mentor"*. Here is a poetry that captures the spirit of a particular time and place, a tapestry of the voices of a people, who are denied a place in that time and have no space in that place.

BELLA

AUTHOR: Isabella Motadinyane
PUBLISHER: Botsotso Publishing

Beginning with the title, **Bella** is a poetry book that repudiates fixed notions of a sense of presence, self and identity and blurs the distinction between being and non-being, past and present and myth and reality. Though **Bella** is short for Isabella this book is not self-titled in the traditional sense of an artist naming his/her work after himself/herself and/or placing himself/herself at the center of his/her work. The choice of this the title is more in the spirit of celebrating the name and personality of Isabella Motadinyane and of remembering and re-membering her life, times and works, rather than a suggestion that the focus of the poems is Isabella Motadinyane. It is true that Isabella passed away in 2004 without having written and published a book. Yet - since **Bella** consists of her works and is named after her - it is also true that Isabella Motadinyane has written a book and has given it her name. The bridging of the chasm between now and then, and between the concrete and the abstract runs like a thread through **Bella.**

The dialogue with the self and the reader is disguised in the form of monologues that contains reminiscent, reflective descriptions of emotions evoked by particular sights and scenes, faces and places, characters, voices and utterances. On the surface it appears as if the object of most of the poems is other characters or certain places but on close scrutiny it turns out that in many instances, one gains more insight into the narrator/poet. In actual fact the poet is finding and expressing herself in her interaction with people and in the enunciation of how others view her. Even where the personal voice of pain and anguish is expressed as in "My Bruised Soul", it is the reaction and utterances of others that movingly capture the poet's fate:

"my night shrieks/ shocks my neighbors/ this is weird/ is she eaten up by rooi mure?/ they cry/ feeling my pain/ my tears/ pulling a sinking boat/ created me pains."

Many of the poems in this collection explore the theme of the intricacy of identity and the fluidity of a sense of self by blurring the line of demarcation between the real and the imagined, the perceptual and the factual, and the abstract and the concrete. Abstract things like shadows, the voice and speech are represented in physical and concrete terms:

"moving shadows thicken on walls/ voices become fluffy/ to listening ears/ i stitched my speech/ to set my back free."

Ironically a strong sense of presence and self is registered in the places the poet/persona has been to, long after s/he's left: *"On a full moon/ under moving shadows/ I left my mark on the floor"*.

The "I" in the poems articulates a self-reflective, soul searching personal voice: *"my bruised soul/ color my face pale/ identity gradually fading/ trying to stretch/ wrinkle lines straight"*, as well as a conversational voice, directed towards both an imaginary audience and a fictional character (or real person): *"You pulled an elastic/ down my legs/ I looked into your eyes."* Relationships and interaction with the other contribute to the growth of a sense of awareness and: *"With the reflections of the moon on your face/ tickling pores of awareness in me/ I spread my sea wings apart/ for you to come in."*

However a handful of poems have the narrative voice that provides commentary on the ills and problems bedeviling society through descriptions of the tragic conditions of the victim: *"she walked a painful lane home/ wiping tears of change/ from her soiled body/ but told one about those fakes/ now her poison intake/ lays her bones / perspires with naked truth."* To highlight the stigma and silence surrounding HIV/AIDS, the poet does not mention the disease throughout the poem but resorts to an English translation of the euphemistic street jargon used to refer to the disease: *"Reading her medical record/ as three little words/ holding back her years"* (In street lingo HIV is often referred to as 'Amaghama amathatho', meaning three letters.)

This beautiful collection of poems, whose only weakness for me is the misspellings and errors in some of the Sesotho/Setswana poems, does justice to the memory and legacy of this great poet.

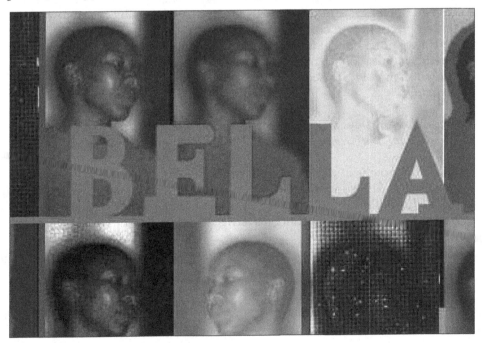

Happy Birthday Saint Mandela; Long-live White privilege!

The schizophrenic selective morality of liberals and conservatives of all shades comes full circle with the psychopathic veneration of Nelson Rolihlahla Mandela while maintaining a rabid hatred for MK operatives like Robert McBride and Andrew Zondo. Mandela is a founder-member of Umkhonto we Sizwe and once answered to the name commander-in-chief and people like McBride and Zondo were mere foot-soldiers carrying out instructions and orders of their command structures. What makes the liberal and conservative establishment to be united in the reverence of Mandela to the point of anointing him a saint while at the same time reserving indignation and bile against a mere mention of the names of McBride, Zondo, Solomon Mahlangu, not to mention cadres of the Azanian People's Liberation Army (APLA) and the Azanian National Liberation Army (AZANLA)?

The same people who shower Mandela with praises for the spirit of forgiveness do not find it in their heart to forgive Robert McBride and Andrew Zondo for the Magoose Bar and the Amazimtoti bombings. The same people who will pat Mandela on the shoulder for visiting Verwoed's wife in Orania (and for calling her the wife of a hero) and would go on about how it is to the benefit of reconciliation that some of the places named after architects and implementers of Apartheid and colonialists should not be changed have a serious problem with the naming of places after Andrew Zondo. In their eyes, Andrew Zondo is just a bloody terrorist.

With due respect to Nelson Mandela, he will be either dumb or egoistic to take seriously accolades given to him by forces who hate the guts of those who - like him - were left with no option but to take up the armed struggle as an avenue to pursue the liberation of their people. As long as they express their intimate love to hate former freedom fighters, the liberals and conservatives give us the reason to believe that their love for Mandela is an expression of appreciation for the role Mandela played in ensuring the creation of a dispensation in which the ownership and control of the land and economy is predominately White. In other words, they embrace a specific phase in the history and life of Mandela and cannot thank Mandela enough for detaching himself completely from a part of his history that is at odds with the agenda of capitalism.

The raging hatred for former MK operatives exposes the fact that it is not Mandela that the liberal and conservative establishment celebrate but rather the successful usage of the Madiba 'aura'\'charisma' to install the reformist and liberalist project in South Africa. It is a celebration of the death and burial of Mandela the ANC Youth League militant and MK commander who believed that the commanding heights of the economy should be public property. It is paying homage the Mandela the free marketeer under whose leadership the ANC to adopted market fundamentalism and assumed GEAR as the key and lock of ANC economic policy despite opposition from the people and workers of the country and their organizations. The deference for Mandela is a show of appreciation for almost single-handedly fighting for the retention of the name and colours of the springbok and for ensuring that the notorious die stem- the anthem of apartheid - is smuggled into Nkosi Sikelela - the anthem of liberation. One can go on….

Remember the times Uncle Sam danced with Uncle Bob?

The political and economic meltdown in Zimbabwe is traceable to the hold on the country's policy alternatives and developmental possibilities by the restraints of the Lancaster House concessions and the constraints of the Structural Adjustment Programmes. Robert Mugabe and his ZANU (PF) implemented these programmes to the letter from 1981 up to 2000. Mugabe and ZANU's reward was the blindness, silence and tacit collusion of the western powers in the genocidal attack on the people of Matabeleland in what is called the Gukurahundi. Despite the fact that Mugabe and Zanu PF continued with the culture of violent clampdown on political dissidence and repression of media freedom and the freedom of association and assembly, the custodians of democracy remained prepared to portray Mugabe as an astute statesman and scrupulous ruler. For as long as he trod the path of the Washington Consensus and cracked his whip against labour and ensured that there was no room for leftists to raise their heads in Zimbabwe, Mugabe could reign on opposition to his rule by any means at his disposal.

Throughout the 1990's, the International Monetary Fund(IMF) and the World Bank and the G8 gave a standing ovation to the social policy path and political economy trajectory pursued by Zimbabwe, South Africa, Uganda and Ethiopia. As late as 2001 political science textbooks at tertiary institutions celebrated Mugabe of Zimbabwe, Mandela of South Africa, Museveni of Uganda, and Zenawi of Ethiopia as the crème de la crème of African leaders, and hailed them as former guerillas who had woken up to the realism of running a country. In 2001 popular disenchantment with the failure to meet liberation expectations and pressure from the war veterans forced the land reform project on the agenda of Mugabe and Zanu PF. Mugabe and Zanu PF then failed dismally to come up with a systematically designed landreform project, with clear targets, performance indicators and monitoring and impact assessment mechanisms. Instead of genuine land reform aimed at sustainable development of communities, they opted for a mixture of anarchist, populist, propagandistic theatrics and bureaucratic centralism, elite' self-enrichment, and the politics of cronyism and patronage aimed at using the land reform project to prop up the power of the establishment.

Suddenly western governments, with the aid of the media and our 'fuckademics' started to shift the focus away from the suffering landless, jobless and poor multitudes of Zimbabwe - who continue to live in utter poverty and squalor - to the fate of white farmers. Both the Western governments and the White farmers in Zimbabwe never raised even a murmur of protest against the rule of Mugabe for as long as their bread remained buttered. All of a sudden, everybody forgot that Mugabe built his repressive machinery under the watchful eyes of the super powers and the so-called multilateral institutions. Nobody cared to remember the role played by the restraints of Lancaster House agreement on a legal-constitutional and peaceful land reform process in Zimbabwe and the ravages of the market forces unleashed by the Structural Adjustment Programmes on the people, economy and environment of Zimbabwe.

Whenever the issue of the war crimes against Mugabe is raised, often the focus is not the crime of the Gukurahundi or the genocidal impoverishment of the people through handing them over to the brutality of the market forces for a decade of subservience to the Washington Consensus. The focus is rather the "crime" of taking land from white farmers. When the Gukurahundi is mentioned no one speaks about the need to also charge Mugabe's main backers throughout this period - the super powers and the Washington institutions - IMF and World Bank. This is not the first time that America and the West, bankrolled and oversaw a one party dictatorship or military rule for decades only to ditch the regime when it is no longer serving their interests. But only after dusting off blood from their hands and clothes, and presenting themselves as the moral voice, urging for war crimes against the very regime that they baby-seated, reared and mentored. From Mobuto Seso Seko, Saddam Hussain, Charles Taylor and the Taliban to Uncle Bob—the list of rulers utilized and dumped like used condoms by Uncle Sam and his brethren is endless. There is no prize if you guess what trajectory Morgan Tsvangirai and his Movement for Democratic Change are most likely to tread if they ascend power. My two year old son, Goitsemodimo, has whispered to me that Zimbabwe will be under the tyranny of the market and remote control by "the empire."

Printed in the United States
By Bookmasters